NEW ESSAYS ON THE AWAKENING

GENERAL EDITOR

Emory Elliott, Princeton University

Other books in the series:
New Essays on The Scarlet Letter
New Essays on The Great Gatsby
New Essays on Adventures of Huckleberry Finn
New Essays on Moby-Dick
New Essays on Uncle Tom's Cabin
New Essays on The Red Badge of Courage
New Essays on The Sun Also Rises
New Essays on The American
New Essays on Light in August
New Essays on Invisible Man

Forthcoming:
New Essays on Wright's Native Son
New Essays on James's The Portrait of a Lady

New Essays on
The Awakening

Edited by
Wendy Martin

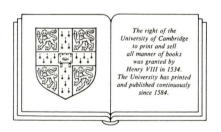

The right of the
University of Cambridge
to print and sell
all manner of books
was granted by
Henry VIII in 1534.
The University has printed
and published continuously
since 1584.

CAMBRIDGE UNIVERSITY PRESS

Cambridge

New York   New Rochelle   Melbourne   Sydney

Published by the Press Syndicate of the University of Cambridge
The Pitt Building, Trumpington Street, Cambridge CB2 1RP
32 East 57th Street, New York, NY 10022, USA
10 Stamford Road, Oakleigh, Melbourne 3166, Australia

First published 1988

Printed in the United States of America

Library of Congress Cataloging-in-Publication Data
New essays on The Awakening / edited by Wendy Martin.
p.   cm. − (The American novel)
Bibliography: p.
Contents: Introduction / Wendy Martin − Tradition and the female
talent : The awakening as a solitary book / Elaine Showalter −
Revolt against nature: the problematic modernism of The awakening /
Michael T. Gilmore − The half-life of Edna Pontellier / Andrew
Delbanco − Edna's wisdom / Cristina Giorcelli.
ISBN 0−521−30712−0. ISBN 0−521−31445−3 (pbk.)
1. Chopin, Kate, 1851−1904. Awakening. [1. Chopin, Kate,
criticism.] I. Martin, Wendy. II. Series.
PS1294.C63A6436   1988
813'4. − dc19   87−30550

British Library Cataloguing in Publication Data
New essays on The awakening. − (The
American novel).
1. Chopin, Kate − Criticism and
interpretation
I. Martin, Wendy II. Series
813'4. PS1294.C632/

ISBN 0 521 30712 0 hard covers
ISBN 0 521 31445 3 paperback

Contents

v

Contents

5
Edna's Wisdom:
A Transitional and Numinous Merging

Series Editor's Preface

In literary criticism the last twenty-five years have been particularly fruitful. Since the rise of the New Criticism in the 1950s, which focused attention of critics and readers upon the text itself—apart from history, biography, and society—there has emerged a wide variety of critical methods which have brought to literary works a rich diversity of perspectives: social, historical, political, psychological, economic, ideological, and philosophical. While attention to the text itself, as taught by the New Critics, remains at the core of contemporary interpretation, the widely shared assumption that works of art generate many different kinds of interpretation has opened up possibilities for new readings and new meanings.

Before this critical revolution, many American novels had come to be taken for granted by earlier generations of readers as having an established set of recognized interpretations. There was a sense among many students that the canon was established and that the larger thematic and interpretative issues had been decided. The task of the new reader was to examine the ways in which elements such as structure, style, and imagery contributed to each novel's acknowledged purpose. But recent criticism has brought these old assumptions into question and has thereby generated a wide variety of original, and often quite surprising, interpretations of the classics, as well as of rediscovered novels such as Kate Chopin's *The Awakening*, which has only recently entered the canon of works that scholars and critics study and that teachers assign their students.

The aim of The American Novel Series is to provide students of American literature and culture with introductory critical guides to

American novels now widely read and studied. Each volume is devoted to a single novel and begins with an introduction by the volume editor, a distinguished authority on the text. The introduction presents details of the novel's composition, publication history, and contemporary reception, as well as a survey of the major critical trends and readings from first publication to the present. This overview is followed by four or five original essays, specifically commissioned from senior scholars of established reputation and from outstanding younger critics. Each essay presents a distinct point of view, and together they constitute a forum of interpretative methods and of the best contemporary ideas on each text.

It is our hope that these volumes will convey the vitality of current critical work in American literature, generate new insights and excitement for students of the American novel, and inspire new respect for and new perspectives upon these major literary texts.

Emory Elliott
Princeton University

1

Introduction

WENDY MARTIN

IN a portrait of Kate Chopin (Katherine O'Flaherty Chopin, 1850–1904), her son Felix remembers her as being available to her three sons and three daughters at all times. Describing his mother as being constantly interrupted by her children as she read or wrote in her Morris chair in the living room that was filled with books and decorated with a few simple paintings, he notes that there was a statue of a naked Venus on one of the bookshelves.[1] This icon of female eros represents the primary concern of Chopin's fiction – the celebration of female sexuality, and the tension between erotic desire and the demands of marriage, the family, and a traditional society.

Kate Chopin juggled the demands of her writing career and motherhood with extraordinary success. Although she often longed for privacy for her work as well as greater personal freedom, she carried out her domestic and social responsibilities with apparent equanimity. In spite of the fact that she was widowed in her early thirties and was left with six children to raise, she established a very comfortable home for her family and was known throughout St. Louis for her thriving household and her salon, which was frequented by the city's most prominent intellectuals and artists. By the mid-1890s, Kate Chopin was a nationally recognized novelist, short story writer, essayist and reviewer. She wrote more than one hundred short stories, many of which were published in *Vogue, The Century,* and the *Atlantic* and were later collected in *Bayou Folk* (1894) and *A Night in Acadie* (1897). Her best-known work, *The Awakening,* was published in 1899.

Born Katherine O'Flaherty in 1850 in St. Louis, Kate Chopin's mother, Eliza Faris, was of French Creole ancestry and her father,

Thomas O'Flaherty, was a prosperous merchant who had emigrated from Ireland in 1825. The O'Flaherty family life was lively, and Kate was a much-loved child. However, when she was four years old, her father was killed by the collapse of the bridge carrying the inaugural train of the Pacific Railroad into St. Louis. After Thomas O'Flaherty's tragic and untimely death, Kate grew close to her maternal grandmother, who spent many hours telling her granddaughter stories of Creole life. The sophisticated plots sometimes involved extramarital romance and interracial marriage, which gave the young girl an unusually complex view of the world.

When Kate O'Flaherty was nine years old, she entered St. Louis Academy of the Sacred Heart. Even though this was her first formal education, she was already an avid reader. Her grandmother's stories had kindled her interest in literature, and she knew all of the French classics as well as *Pilgrim's Progress, Grimm's Fairy Tales, Ivanhoe,* and much of Dickens. As she grew older she became increasingly sophisticated in her taste, and read Dante, Cervantes, Goethe, Coleridge, Austen, and the Brontës as well. After graduating from the Academy in June 1868, she continued to be a voracious reader and became especially interested in the work of Madame de Stael. An entry in her commonplace book records a conversation between Byron and de Stael that explores the relationship between passion and virtue in their respective works. Apparently, the young student was fascinated by the fact that Byron – of all people – accused de Stael of undermining the morals of young women with her tales of unrequited love. During her late adolescence, Kate O'Flaherty had an active social life that included parties and balls, picnics, and the theater; at the same time, she felt guilty for spending so much of her time with social amusements. When she met Oscar Chopin, who was then twenty-five, she fell in love with the young French Creole from northwestern Louisiana – Natchitoches – and agreed to marry him.[2]

After a three-month European honeymoon, Oscar and Kate Chopin moved to New Orleans, where she spent considerable time exploring the city, which seemed more Old World than American to her. The couple lived in New Orleans for nine years until excessive rain ruined the cotton industry in 1878–9. They then moved their large family to Cloutierville. Chopin describes the little town as a "French village" consisting of "two long rows of very old frame houses, facing each other closely across a dusty highway." Apparently, she lived a reasonably contented life there and is described as being a gracious hostess with considerable leisure and enough time to travel to St. Louis for lengthy visits. When Oscar caught swamp fever – malaria – in 1883 and died suddenly, the thirty-three-year-old Kate Chopin took over the management of the Natchitoches plantation and directed the enterprise with considerable success. But after a year, she sold the business and moved her family back to St. Louis to be closer to her mother. However, this reunion was very brief; Mrs. O'Flaherty died in June 1885, and the loss of husband and mother in rapid succession was devastating. Kate Chopin's daughter describes her mother as sinking into a depression from which she probably never fully recovered: "I think the tragic death of her father early in her life . . . the loss of her young husband and her mother, left a stamp of sadness on her which was never lost."[3]

Chopin's obstetrician, Frederick Kolbenheyer, was one of the few people who seemed to understand her during the period following the deaths of her husband and mother. He was an intellectual who was respected in St. Louis for his knowledge of philosophy and contemporary scientific theory, especially the work of Kant, Hegel, and Schopenhauer, as well as Darwin, Huxley, and Spencer. Noting that Chopin was articulate and had descriptive abilities, Kolbenheyer urged her to write; he understood that writing could be a focus for her extraordinary energy, as well as a source of income. His influence on his patient was profound, so much so that Kate Chopin gave up her Catholic faith and embarked on a career as a writer. At first she wrote love poetry lamenting her husband's death; these poems were extremely sentimental but were nevertheless published in *America*, a literary magazine located in Chicago in 1889. At this time, she also began writing short stories and was deeply influenced by the work of Maupassant, whom she credited with teaching her how to write:

> I had been in the woods, in the fields, groping around; looking for something big, satisfying, convincing . . . [when] I stumbled upon Maupassant. I read his stories and marvelled at them. Here

3

was life, not fiction; for where were the plots, the old fashioned mechanism and stage trapping that in a vague, unthinking way I had fancied were essential to the art of story making. Here was a man who had escaped from tradition and authority, who had entered into himself and looked out upon life through his own being and with his own eyes; and who, in a direct and simple way, told us what he saw.[4]

What Chopin valued in Maupassant, then, was his skillful rendering of subjective experience and his emphasis on the importance of individual consciousness.

Chopin also read and admired Sarah Orne Jewett, Mary Wilkins Freeman, and William Dean Howells and wrote a short story, "A Poor Girl," in an attempt to achieve the realistic texture that was characteristic of their work. This story was not accepted for publication but two others, "Wiser Than a God" and "A Point at Issue," were published in 1889. Both of these works explore the tension between artistic aspiration and social convention. In 1890, Chopin completed a novel, "At Fault," which she published and promoted at her own expense. Again, she explores the themes of emotional autonomy and the moral constraints imposed by society. Even though this first novel was published by a vanity press, it received a surprising number of reviews — including one in *The Nation*. Most of the reviewers objected to what they considered the questionable morals of the characters but admired its descriptive power and skillful characterizations.

Reinforced by the praise of "At Fault," Chopin completed another novel, "Young Dr. Gosse," two years later but failed to find a publisher for it. Turning to short fiction, she wrote at least forty stories, portraits, and vignettes that were published in local journals during the next three years. In 1893 Chopin's stories began to appear in Eastern magazines; the next eight years, *Vogue* accepted eighteen of her stories for publication. Most of her stories continued to explore the tension between emotional and erotic inclination and traditional social mores; for example, "A Shameful Affair," "A Lady of Bayou St. John," and "At Chenière Caminada" are unabashed explorations of eros and its consequences. Chopin's willingness to wrestle with taboo issues was unusual in a woman writer of her generation and earned her a reputation for striking boldness.

In May 1893, Chopin went to New York City to interest publishers in her second novel and in a collection of her short stories, and Houghton Mifflin agreed to publish *Bayou Folk*. Because this volume, published in 1894, consisted of twenty-three stories that take place in Louisiana, for the most part Natchitoches, Chopin earned the reputation of being an important new local color writer. However, several reviews, especially those in *The Nation* and the *St. Louis Post-Dispatch*, also praised her wider vision and stylistic expertise that transcended regional circumstances.[5] Encouraged by the attention her work received, Chopin wrote the truly daring "The Story of an Hour" in April 1894. The story describes the complex and certainly untraditional response of a woman who receives the news that her husband has been killed in a railroad accident; she weeps profusely and then exults that she is now unencumbered: "free, free, free!" she exclaims. The narration elaborates Louise Mallard's excitement:

> She did not stop to ask if it were or were not a monstrous joy that held her. A clear and exalted perception enabled her to dismiss the suggestion as trivial. . . . She saw a long procession of years to come that would belong to her absolutely. And she opened and spread her arms out to them in welcome.
> There would be no one to live for her during those coming years; she would live for herself. There would be no powerful will bending hers in that blind persistence with which men and women believe that they have a right to impose a private will upon a fellow-creature.[6]

Embedded in this text is an extremely radical, even subversive, view of the institution of patriarchal marriage and family, in which the power is traditionally held by husbands, not by wives and certainly not by children.

Apparently, this story signaled a more assertive phase of Kate Chopin's development as a person and as a writer. In less than a decade she had published a novel, nearly one hundred stories and numerous sketches, essays, poems, and a one-act comedy, as well as having written a second novel that remained unpublished. A diary entry dated about a month after she completed "The Story of an Hour" indicates that she was pleased with her accomplishments and was living very much in the present:

> How curiously the past effaces itself for me! I sometimes regret that it is so; for there must be a certain pleasure in retrospection. I cannot live through yesterday or tomorrow. It is why the dead in their character of dead and association with the grave have no hold upon me. . . . If it were possible for my husband and my mother to come back to earth, I feel that I would unhesitatingly give up every thing that has come into my life since they left it and join my existence again with theirs. To do that, I would have to forget the past ten years of my growth – my real growth. But I would take back a little wisdom with me: it would be the spirit of perfect acquiescence.[7]

Clearly, Chopin loved the freedom she had to pursue her own interests, and the theme of freedom from binding responsibility recurs in many of her stories. One of the most striking examples of this preoccupation is "A Pair of Silk Stockings," in which the female protagonist, Mrs. Sommers, longs to escape her responsibility to her children. In an afternoon of abandon, she treats herself to a luxurious lunch, the cinema, elegant gloves, and a pair of silk stockings. Other stories, such as "A Sentimental Soul" and "Madame Celestin's Divorce," are also excellent examples of the tension between self-effacement and self-assertion that is characteristic of Chopin's work.

Many of the stories that were published in her second collection, *A Night in Acadie,* in 1897 continue to explore female sexuality and the lives of women who follow (or would like to follow) their erotic impulses. The heroine of "Athenaise" acts out of passion; Madame Farival of "Lilacs" has several affairs; Suzima in "A Vocation and a Voice" takes a young boy as a lover; and Alberta of "Two Portraits" has sexual liaisons "when and where she chooses." Unlike most of her literary contemporaries, Chopin does not moralize about her heroines' moral frailty. More important, she does not attempt to make her fiction acceptable by punishing her heroines for their unconventional sexuality. Frequently, she had difficulty publishing her stories because of her amoral style; R. W. Gilder refused to publish "The Story of an Hour" in *Century* magazine because he thought it was unethical. Even when Chopin toned down her work in an effort to appear in *Century* magazine (the protagonists in "A No-Account Creole" and "A Night in Acadie" were both chastened for flaunting convention), Gilder refused to publish them. However, when H. E. Scudder, the editor who accepted "Athenaise" for the *Atlantic,* suggested that she write another novel, she began work on *The Awakening.* Two years later, in April 1899, it was published by Herbert S. Stone & Company of Chicago and New York.

In recent years, critics have generally acknowledged the importance of *The Awakening* as an effectively crafted narrative of Edna Pontellier's conflict between individual autonomy and social conformity, but the reviewers in the period immediately following publication of the novel condemned Chopin's protagonist as weak, selfish, and immoral; most of them smugly gloated over her suicide. Frances Porcher announced in the May 4, 1899, issue of *The Mirror* that Edna has "awakened to know the shifting, treacherous, fickle deeps of her own soul in which lies, alert and strong and cruel, the fiend called Passion, that is all animal and all of earth, earthy." Porcher concluded her review: "It is better to lie down in the green waves and sink down in close embraces of old ocean, and so she does."[8] Six weeks later the reviewer in *Public Opinion* announced: "we are all well satisfied when Mrs. Pontellier deliberately swims out to her death in the waters of the gulf."[9] Another review that appeared at the same time in *Literature* describes the novel as an "essentially vulgar" story and concluded, "the waters of the gulf close appropriately over one who has drifted from all right moorings, and has not the grace to repent."[10] The reviewer of the *Providence Sunday Journal,* who singled out Chopin's novel for the "Book of the Week" section, announced, "Miss Kate Chopin is another clever woman, but she has put her cleverness to a very bad use in writing *The Awakening.* The purport of the story can hardly be described in language fit for publication."[11] And the reviewer from the *Los Angeles Sunday Times* complained, "the novel is unhealthily introspective and morbid in feeling . . . when she writes another book it is to be hoped that she will choose a theme more healthful and sweeter of smell."[12] The reviewer from the *St. Louis Daily Globe-Democrat,* proclaiming the book "unhealthy," objected to the fact that the book had no particular moral or lesson to teach but nevertheless admitted that the book handled "a problem that obtrudes itself only too frequently in the social life of people with whom the question of food and clothing is not the all absorbing one."[13] C. L. Deyo in the *St. Louis Post-Dispatch* said that the novel was for "seasoned souls," not for young readers; "it is sad and mad and bad, but it is all consummate art."[14] The *Chicago Times-Herald* chastised Chopin for entering "the overworked field of sex fiction."[15] The *New Orleans Times-Democrat* berated Chopin for failing to condemn her heroine's behavior: "nowhere [is there] a single note of censure of her totally unjustifiable conduct." This reviewer was particularly disturbed by the fact that Chopin seemed to condone extramarital involvement and chose the expression of individual preference over familial responsibility:

> In a civilized society the right of the individual to indulge all his caprices is, and must be, subject to many restrictive clauses, and it cannot for a moment be admitted that a woman who has accepted the love and devotion of a man, even without equal love on her part – who has become his wife and the mother of his children – has not incurred a moral obligation which peremptorily forbids her from wantonly severing her relations with him, and entering openly upon the independent existence of an unmarried woman.[16]

The prominence of double negatives in the preceding quotation reveals the reviewer's defensive uncertainty, as well as his effort to build linguistic bulwarks to shore up eroding traditions. Even Willa Cather, who was then a young journalist for the *The Pittsburgh Leader*, described the novel as a "Creole Bovary" and complained that Edna Pontellier and Emma Bovary "both belong to a class, not large, but forever clamoring in our ears, that demands more romance out of life than God puts into it."[17] The *St. Louis Republic* denounced *The Awakening* as "too strong drink for moral babes, and should be labeled 'poison.'"[18]

The flood of reviews condemning the book eventually led to its being banned by the Mercantile and St. Louis Public Libraries. In addition, Kate Chopin was shunned by many people who had formerly attended her literary receptions, and she was not admitted to the St. Louis Artists' Guild. Chopin did have an opportunity to answer her critics in the "Aims and Autographs of Authors" section of *Book News* in July 1899, in which she wrote a brief paragraph that has often been construed as a retraction but that is more likely to have been intended as an ironic commentary on the narrow-minded response to her novel:

> Having a group of people at my disposal, I thought it might be entertaining (to myself) to throw them together and see what would happen. I never dreamed of Mrs. Pontellier making such a mess of things and working out her own damnations as she did. If I had the slightest intimation of such a thing I would have excluded her from the company. But when I found out what she was up to, the play was half over and it was then too late.[19]

Chopin's disclaimer of responsibility for the controversial contents of *The Awakening* is a tactic often used by women to ward off hostile reviewers. Feigned innocence and conspicuous naiveté are traditional feminine gambits to gain the protection of men.

Among the papers in the Chopin collection at the Missouri Historical Society are letters from Lady Janet Scammon Young and Dr. Dunrobin Thompson that may not in fact be genuine (no scholar has ever been able to authenticate the documents, and in fact they could have been written by Chopin herself). Nevertheless, these letters are significant because they illuminate Chopin's intentions for her novel. The letter from Lady Young is dated October 5, 1899 (a few months after Chopin's disclaimer appeared in *Book News*), and bears a London address. In addition to affirming Chopin's exploration of female sexuality, it is a remarkable exposition on the nature of women's erotic impulses. In an imaginary reworking of Dr. Mandelet's advice to Leonce Pontellier, Young is quite emphatic in her insistence that women be perceived as passionate beings, not as sexless, ethereal creatures: "No woman comes to her full womanly empire and charm who has not felt . . . the arousing power of more than one man."[20] But, Young adds, it is essential that women learn to distinguish between sexual attraction and love, an impossible goal if female consciousness continues to be distorted by the ideal of female passionlessness that prevailed in the nineteenth century. Similarly, the letter written by Dr. Thompson counsels husbands to accept their wives' capacity for sexual pleasure and to celebrate this erotic potential, not condemn female desire as impure. These views were unusually advanced for Chopin's society;

certainly the reviewers of *The Awakening* — for the most part, traditional men — did not share this perspective.

In an essay, "Reflection," that Chopin wrote for the *Post-Dispatch* on November 26, 1899, during the discouraging period after the publication of *The Awakening*, she expressed her disappointment that *The Awakening* was not given more serious attention and that the libraries had banned it, lamenting that the "moving procession . . . [has] left me by the roadside."[21] She continued to write in spite of the adverse reception of *The Awakening*; however, additional rejection further disheartened her. "Ti Demon," a narrative of a young woman's insistence on her right to flirt with whomever she pleases, was rejected by the *Atlantic* for being too "sombre." (This story is clearly Chopin's defense of her own artistic and social autonomy.) In February 1900 her collection of stories, *A Vocation and a Voice*, was rejected by Herbert Stone of the Stone and Kimball publishing company. This must have been extremely painful for her because she had been able to place her previous short story collections easily. The story — "Charlie" — that Chopin wrote in April 1900, just after these rejections, indirectly expresses her anger about the repression of female energy and the criticism of women's accomplishments. This story reveals Chopin's considerable hostility toward those critics who had chastised her for permitting her female protagonists to take the liberties that men have traditionally had. Charlie is a young woman who likes to wear boots and pants, tote guns, and manage her father's plantation. One day, while brandishing her gun to coerce the men on her father's farm to work, she shoots a young man in the arm. The embedded message in this text — the wounding and disabling of a man — expresses the rage and the desire for retaliation Chopin must have felt in the face of the negative reaction to *The Awakening* by male critics as well as to the wounding of her capacity for self-assertion. When Charlie's gun is taken away and she is forced to give up her masculine clothes, she submits to the injunction that she behave like a proper young woman. This retreat into modesty is the penalty for female aggression. But the plot takes another ironic turn when her father loses his arm in a railroad accident and she is given the responsibility of running the plantation for him; in effect, Charlie becomes her father's right-hand man. Once again, she wears boots and pants, carries a gun, and functions extremely effectively as a manager. By having her heroine reclaim her assertive role, Chopin signals a refusal to submit to patriarchal authority. In spite of this aggressive stance, however, two of the four stories that concluded Chopin's career could be construed as capitulation; the heroines are career women who are happy to exchange their work as teacher and bookkeeper for the "labor of loving." Whether this retreat into domesticity represents artistic defeat or simply an effort to please conservative editors, we will never know.

In the years following the publication of *The Awakening*, Kate Chopin's health began to fail. Although she was only in her early fifties, she felt weak and needed an unusual amount of rest. In many respects, her invalidism was a somatic enactment of her diminished status as a writer. During the St. Louis World's Fair in 1904, she seemed more like her old self and visited the exposition frequently. After a particularly long day at the fair, she suffered a brain hemorrhage and died two days later. One of her biographers, Per Seyersted, has observed that "The great achievement of Kate Chopin was that she broke new ground in American literature. She was the first woman writer in her country to accept passion as a legitimate subject for serious, outspoken fiction . . . she undertook to give the unsparing truth about a woman's submerged life."[22]

Chopin's first biographer, Daniel Rankin, indicates that *The Awakening* sold well, but he seems to have been whistling in the dark. In fact, Chopin received practically no royalties for the novel: $109 in 1899, $40 in 1900, and $3 in 1901.[23] It was republished in 1906, when rights to the novel were transferred to Duffield & Company. But as a 1910 article on Chopin and *The Awakening* that appeared in the *St. Louis Republic* observes, Chopin was a writer who was ahead of her time. After the initial round of disapproving reviews the book was ignored, and it was another fifty years before it received the attention it deserved.

American critics and literary scholars generally did not mention *The Awakening* in the standard literary histories. For example, Fred Lewis Patee left Chopin out of the *Cambridge History of American Literature*, published in 1918; this is not surprising in view of his extremely brief mention of her in his *History of American Literature*

Since 1870, published in 1915. However, in *The Development of the American Short Story,* published in 1923, Patee observes that a few of her short stories are "masterpieces" that should earn her the status of "genius, taut, vibrant, intense of soul."[24] The Chopin entry for the 1930 *Dictionary of American Biography,* written by Dorothy Anne Dondore, singles out the short story "Desiree's Baby" as an extraordinary accomplishment. Praising *The Awakening* as a sophisticated, carefully crafted novel, Dondore observes that "one of the tragedies of recent American literature [is] that Mrs. Chopin should have written this book two decades in advance of its time."[25]

Daniel Rankin published the first biography of Kate Chopin in 1932 but has no sympathy for *The Awakening,* which he criticizes for its "erotic morbidity."[26] Arthur Hobson Quinn also describes the novel as "morbid."[27] When Chopin is mentioned in literary histories, she is generally categorized as a local color writer, as she was by Carlos Baker in the 1948 edition of the *Literary History of the United States.*[28] However, a French critic, Cyrille Arnavon, grouped her with realist writers like Frank Norris and Theodore Dreiser, rather than with George Washington Cable, Joel Chandler Harris, Sarah Orne Jewett, and Mary Wilkins Freeman, who have been traditionally described as regional writers. Declaring *The Awakening* to be a realistic novel, Arnavon compared it to *Madame Bovary,* and in 1953 he published a French translation of the novel accompanied by a lengthy discussion of its importance as a realistic treatment of sex and marriage.[29] Echoing Arnavon, Clarence Gohdes also likened *The Awakening* to *Madame Bovary;* a year later, in *The Confident Years 1885–1915* (1952), Van Wyck Brooks admitted that *The Awakening* was "one novel of the nineties in the South that should have been remembered, one small perfect book that mattered more than the whole life-work of many a prolific writer."[30] In *Patriotic Gore: Studies in the Literature of the American Civil War* (1962), Edmund Wilson described the novel as "quite uninhibited and beautifully written, which anticipates D. H. Lawrence in its treatment of infidelity."[31] Deeper interest in Kate Chopin's work in general, and in *The Awakening* in particular, was stimulated by Per Seyersted's critical biography, published in 1969, as well as his edition of her collected works, published in the same year. Recently, there has been widespread interest in the novel; it certainly holds an established place in the canon of American literature, and it is frequently assigned as required reading in surveys of American literature, as well as in courses on American women writers.

Kenneth Eble, Larzar Ziff, Per Seyersted, and Lewis Leary have all observed that *The Awakening* is noteworthy for its unusual candor about female sexuality. Praising the novel for its thoughtful exploration of the problem of a woman's erotic needs in a repressed society, Larzar Ziff writes in *The American 1890's: Life and Times of a Lost Generation* that the novel

> was the most important piece of fiction about the sexual life of a woman written to date in America, and the first fully to face the fact that marriage, whether in point of fact it closed the range of woman's sexual experiences or not, was but an episode in her continuous growth . . . on the very eve of the twentieth century it raised the question of what woman was to do with the freedom she struggled toward.[32]

Kenneth Eble describes *The Awakening* as "a first-rate novel," praising it for its "general excellence." Per Seyersted also notes that Chopin's treatment of female sexuality is more complete and "more convincing" than that of any other American novelist to date, and he praises the fundamental seriousness of the novel.[33] Lewis Leary notes that "Mrs. Chopin has presented a compelling portrait of a trapped and finally desperate woman, a drama of self-discovery, of awakening and doom, a tragedy perhaps of self-deceit."[34]

Edna Pontellier's suicide has received considerable attention. Several critics comment on the price of freedom as Chopin portrays Edna Pontellier's fate: Jules Chametzky observes that "it is a lonely and isolated autonomy that exacts a terrible price"; Donald Ringe notes that "the philosophic questions raised by Edna's awakening [are] the relation of the individual self to the physical and social realities by which it is surrounded, and the price it must pay for insisting upon absolute freedom."[35] George Arms views Edna's suicide as a passive drifting and asserts that she is the victim of her own self-delusion.[36] George Spangler sees the conclusion of the novel as being at odds with Edna Pontellier's essential strength and asserts that the conclusion represents a sentimental lapse on Chopin's part.[37] Writing from a psychoanalytic perspective, Cynthia Griffin Wolff observes that Edna's suicide is a regressive act that is the result of arrested emotional development. According to Wolff, Edna experiences "an inner sense of emptiness" that no adult relationship can remedy.[38] As we have seen, many contemporary critics and students romanticize Edna's suicide as an act of self-assertion, as a transcendence of her earthly limitations. Donald Ringe describes Edna's death as a "defeat that involves no surrender."[39] Other critics focus on the ambiguous nature of the suicide: Ruth Sullivan, Stewart Smith, and Kenneth Rosen argue that the conclusion of the novel underscores the essential ambivalence of Edna's nature. On the one hand, she is a romantic absolutist and will not compromise her vision of freedom; on the other, she is defeated by convention.[40] Suzanne Wolkenfeld points out that "Edna's suicide is not a conscious choice reached through her achievement of self-awareness."[41] Margaret Culley interprets Edna's drowning as a kind of liberation from the confining network of social relationships in which a woman is defined "as someone's daughter, someone's wife, someone's mother, someone's mistress."[42] Clearly, contemporary evaluations of the novel vary markedly in their assessment of the effectiveness of its conclusion, but most critics today agree that *The Awakening* is an important part of the American literary canon.

The lush prose and sensuous imagery of *The Awakening* represent a dramatic departure from the technique and point of view found in other contemporary novels about women such as Theodore Dreiser's *Sister Carrie*. However, like Chopin, Dreiser was attacked by critics because he wrote candidly about marital discord and divorce; indeed, the wife of Dreiser's publisher almost prevented the publication of *Sister Carrie* altogether because Carrie wasn't sufficiently punished at the end of the novel. Both novelists probe the severely limited lives of women at the turn of the century, but Chopin's study is more evocative, more richly detailed in regard to the actual experience of the post-Victorian woman. A comparison of the language of the representative passages from the two novels reveals essential differences in style and perspective:

And now Carrie attained that which in the beginning seems life's object, or, at least, such a fraction of it as human beings ever attain of their original desires. She could look about on her gowns and carriage, her furniture and bank account. Friends there were . . . and yet she was lonely.[43]

The golden shimmer of Edna's satin gown spread in rich folds on either side of her. There was a soft fall of lace encircling her shoulders. It was the color of her skin, without the glow, the myriad living tints that one may sometimes discover in the vibrant flesh. . . . But as she sat there amid her guests, she felt the old ennui overtaking her, the hopelessness which so often assailed her. (Chap. 30)

Chopin's language is more vibrant: emphasizing colors, textures, the quality of light, her prose has a sensuous richness that Dreiser's lacks. In general, the reader has a more intimate understanding of Edna's emotions because they are experienced in a subjective, tactile content. The reader participates in Edna's alienation and boredom but is told in a declarative statement that Carrie is lonely.

Other representative passages convey the visual and textural richness — the synesthetic blend of sights and sounds — that resonates throughout *The Awakening*:

There were wax candles in massive brass candelabra, burning softly under yellow silk shades; full, fragrant roses, yellow and red abounded. There were silver and gold . . . and crystal which glittered like the gems which the women wore. . . . Before each guest stood a tiny glass that looked and sparkled like a garnet gem (Chap. 30)

The stillest hour of the night had come, the hour before the dawn, when the world seems to hold its breath. The moon hung low, and had turned from silver to copper, in the sleeping sky. The old owl no longer hooted, and the water oaks ceased to moan as they bent their heads. (Chap. 11)

As nature's cycles and rhythms are contemplated in the novel, so are the needs of the body as Edna becomes increasingly aware of her erotic impulses, first toward Robert, then toward Arobin. Written during a period of extreme sexual repression, especially of women of the middle and upper classes, it is not surprising that the novel shocked conventional reviewers. In general, proper women were not perceived as having sexual needs or as being capable of experiencing erotic pleasures or orgasm. For a respectable woman, the sex act was one of self-sacrifice; the true woman was passionless. Because birth control was uncertain at best, and death from the complications of numerous pregnancies or in childbirth itself was frequent, it is not surprising that many women associated sex with pain rather than pleasure.

New Orleans, the general setting for *The Awakening*, was known for its European sophistication and worldliness, but the sexuality that was expected, or even demanded, of women of color was not tolerated in their Caucasian counterparts. Harriet Martineau's descriptions of the quadroon and octoroon women who were trained as concubines of the planters or wealthy merchants indicate the racist and sexist double standard that prevailed in the South, where skin color was elaborately graduated. Color charts that hung in drugstores and other public buildings provided an extremely complex key to the hierarchical ranking of racial ancestry. Moral qualities were attributed to degrees of skin pigmentation, and black women were condemned as lustful she-devils while white women were praised for ethereal purity akin to that of the angels.

In addition to the racist and sexist values of the patriarchal South, there was a general acceptance of the notion of separate spheres for men and women. The public sphere belonged to men, and women were assigned to the private sphere of domestic life. Psychological attributes were also neatly bifurcated. Men were associated with reason, objectivity, the law; women with emotion, subjectivity, and ritual. Feminine virtue was encoded in the private sphere. As a respectable woman, Edna violates social mores by appearing in public with Arobin, a man of questionable reputation. The strict rules governing feminine propriety in New Orleans are outlined in an article that appeared in *The Chautauquan* in 1892 warning women to be exceedingly careful in the selection of friends.[44] This cautionary advice was especially pertinent to Creole women, the descendants of the French and Spanish born in Louisiana. Although Edna was not a Creole, her husband was, and she was expected to honor his traditions. Kate Chopin's bold accomplishment in creating a character who tries to break through the paralyzing code of feminine purity and entangling web of custom that constricted women's lives gives *The Awakening* historical importance as well as social interest. But the novel is not simply about the sexual awakening of a woman in traditional society. It is about the emerging individuality of a woman who refuses to be defined by the prevailing stereotypes of passive femininity but who lacks the psychological resources and training to resist the tradition of enforced passivity.

In many respects, *The Awakening* is about death, not life. Edna Pontellier's struggle for selfhood is doomed because there is little possibility for self-determination for women in a society where legal and economic practice and social custom prohibit female autonomy. At the turn of the century, when *The Awakening* was published, marriage in New Orleans was based on the Napoleonic Code, which defined a wife and everything she possessed, including her clothes, as her husband's property. Divorce was an infrequent and scandalous event, particularly in Louisiana, which was a Catholic state. In 1890 there were only 29 divorces per 100,000 population, and until 1888 the custody of children was automatically given to the husband.[45]

The depth of southern antagonism toward female emancipation is revealed in a treatise on the growth of suffragism spawned by the Civil War published in 1891, in which Wilbur Fisk Tillet insists that the women's movement will make no headway in the region:

> So far as this movement may have any tendency to take woman out of her true place in the home, to give her man's work to do and to develop masculine qualities in her, it finds no sympathy in the South. The Southern woman loves the retirement of home, and shrinks from everything that would bring her into the public gaze.[46]

In addition to outlining the terms of true womanhood that women of all classes were supposed to accept as an ideal, Tillet's elaboration of the separation of masculine and feminine spheres reiterates the equation of femininity with domestic experience and masculinity with public life. For the traditionalist, the differentiation of duties and interests along gender lines was supposed to reduce competition between the sexes by providing men and women with separate territories. However, this psychological division of labor, described as complementarity, often resulted in social and psychological fragmentation, exacerbating rather than minimizing tension.

Charlotte Perkins Gilman understood the psychological cost to women of domestic seclusion and denounced the channeling of female energy into the service of what she considered to be a waning tradition. In *Women and Economics,* published one year before *The Awakening,* Gilman ridiculed the excesses of home worship: "The home is the centre and circumference, the start and the finish, of most of our lives. . . . We reverence it with the blind obeisance of those crouching centuries when its cult began."[47] In 1891, Gilman had published *The Yellow Wallpaper,* a narrative of a wife's nervous breakdown from excessive confinement to the domestic sphere. The story is an autobiographical account of Gilman's rest cure, prescribed by Dr. Silas Weir Mitchell, who became famous for prescribing total inactivity for women with emotional problems. In addition to bed rest and complete isolation, Weir's patients were given an all-milk diet combined with bland foods. Not surprisingly, women who were bored, restless, or anxiety-ridden from inadequate contact with the world outside the home were made even more so by Dr. Mitchell's regimen. Gilman understood the dangers of domestic seclusion, and she satirized the traditions that she felt endangered the mental and physical health of women:

> And since we hold that our home life, just as we have it, is the best thing on earth, and that our home life plainly demands the whole woman at least to each home, and usually more, it follows that anything which offers to change the position of women threatens to "undermine the home," "strikes at the root of the family," and we will have none of it.[48]

The nurturing function and decorative value of the middle- and upper-class woman was analyzed in depth in Thorstein Veblen's now classic study, *The Theory of the Leisure Class,* published in the same year as *The Awakening.* Veblen argues that the Industrial Revolution resulted in a widening gap between the leisured and working classes: In the aristocracy, both men and women have considerable discretionary time whereas this luxury is unavailable to either sex in the working class. Having neither the financial resources of the privileged class nor the harsh necessity of the working class, the middle class divides the activities of work and play along gender lines. Through his industry, the middle-class husband produces the wealth necessary for his wife to consume the goods and services traditionally available to the privileged class. In Veblen's analysis, then, the function of the wife in a financially comfortable middle-class marriage is largely ceremonial; through her conspicuous consumption of leisure, she confers status on her husband.

Certainly Veblen's theory provides insight into the lives of the women who summer at Grand Isle, an island fifty miles off the Louisiana coast in the Gulf of Mexico, while their husbands work in New Orleans and visit their families on weekends. The quintessential "good husband," Leonce Pontellier provides a luxurious life for his family. While away on business, he sends Edna a box of delicacies — "the finest of fruits, pates, a rare bottle or two, delicious syrups, and bonbons in abundance" (Chap. 3) — as a sign of his status as a good provider. In a highly ritualized gesture that underscores her husband's economic prowess, Edna shares his gift with the other wives, who, in turn, ritually proclaim Mr. Pontellier "the best husband in the world" (Chap. 3). Edna also displays her husband's wealth by dressing well and by being a gracious and generous hostess. When she violates these expectations — for example, when she refuses to entertain her weekly visitors — she dishonors her husband. Interestingly, Leonce Pontellier responds to Edna's psychological upheaval by stressing financial concerns: "You can't afford to snub Mrs. Belthrop. Why, Belthrop could buy and sell us ten times over" (Chap. 17). Pragmatic demands shape emotions in Mr. Pontellier's world. Even Edna's physical being is subject to his scrutiny and approval. For example, when she becomes sunburned, he reacts as though the temporary marring of her skin is an asset lost: Leonce Pontellier is described as "looking at his wife as one looks at a valuable piece of personal property which has suffered some damage" (Chap. 1).

Edna Pontellier is not comfortable with the traditional role of wife and mother but has difficulty imagining alternatives. Anticipating Virginia Woolf's description of the "angel in the house," Chopin describes the "mother woman" as being thoroughly self-sacrificing: "They were women who idolized their children, wor-

19

shipped their husbands, and esteemed it a holy privilege to efface themselves as individuals and grow wings, as ministering angels" (Chap. 4). The conflict between self-sacrifice and self-realization is intense for Edna. But instead of doing needlework with Adele Ratignolle, Edna accepts the invitation of the sea to "wander . . . in abysses of solitude; to lose [herself] in mazes of inward contemplation" (Chap. 6). By rejecting the centrality of domestic life, Edna gives up the social and economic scenario that provides the basis for her existence. By stepping out of the protected space of home, which in the nineteenth century was imbued with an almost religious sanctity, Edna experiences an exhilarating sense of possibility and frightening uncertainty. Like the sea, this freedom is thrilling but perilous.

That romantic love should be the catalyst for Edna's desire for selfhood is paradoxical but nevertheless important. The summer colony at Grand Isle, as Sandra Gilbert suggests, is a colony of women and children.[49] This female community shares, for the most part, a cohesive Roman Catholic Creole culture. As a Presbyterian – an American Protestant – Edna does not participate in the social rituals of that society. For Creole women, romance is simply an aristocratic amusement, much as it was in the court of Eleanor of Aquitaine. But for Edna, the romantic mode is a substitute for religion; the beloved is exalted to divine status and perceived as having redemptive power. The "young Robert Lebrun," as Leonce Pontellier refers to him, is almost a religious presence in Edna's consciousness; the more geographically distant he is, the more he compels her emotions. The dominant trope of romantic love is the longing and unfulfilled desire. Passion is perceived as essentially a passive emotion; the depth of passion is characterized by intense preoccupation with the beloved and by an overwhelming sense of being engulfed by the beloved. Traditionally, passion entails suffering – the passion of Christ being the exemplary model. Romantic agony, in fact, is a secularized version of Gethsemane. But as Nina Baym points out, Edna's sexual "enthrallment" is "finally another impediment to absolute freedom."[50]

In his biography of Kate Chopin, Per Seyersted notes that the original title for *The Awakening* was *A Solitary Self*.[51] Yet, in spite of her yearning for autonomy, the futility of Edna Pontellier's attempts to define herself as being separate from her family is built into the language of the novel by the pervasive use of the passive voice to describe Edna's experience. The syntax of the novel underscores the fact that Edna is trapped and defeated by the cultural edict of passive femininity, which she has internalized to such an extent that even her own emotions are perceived as forces that drive her. For example, her depression is described as engulfing her: "An indescribable oppression which seemed to generate in some unfamiliar part of her consciousness, filled her being with anguish. It was like a shadow, like a mist passing across her soul's summer day" (Chap. 3).

Edna does not want to give primacy to nurturing; she will not serve others, but she cannot serve herself. Her life represents the tension between Adele Ratignolle's code of affiliation and the politics of separation of Madame Reisz. Often Edna's life seems like a montage of dreams; emotions surface, and she drifts on a sea of impressions. She does not look at the world with purpose, definition, or focus. She has a "sensuous susceptibility to beauty" (Chap. 7): Music arouses "passions within her soul, swaying it, lashing it"; her body "fell into splendid poses" (Chap. 7); "a subtle current of desire passed through her body, weakening her hold upon the brushes and making her eyes burn" (Chap. 19); "she was still under the spell of her infatuation . . . the thought of him was like an obsession ever pressing itself upon her" (Chap. 18). Her marriage is described as "purely an accident," "a decree of fate." When asked what she is thinking about, she replies, "I was really not conscious of thinking of anything, but perhaps I can retrace my thoughts" (Chap. 7). Hers is the realm of the unconscious, the subjective, of receptivity and reverie – characteristics traditionally ascribed to the female psyche.

Edna is entwined in daydreams, lost in process; she says, "Sometimes I feel . . . as if I were walking through a green meadow again, idly, aimlessly, unthinking and unguided" (Chap. 7). On the one hand, she is Rousseau's child of nature; on the other, she is confined to sensibility and lacks the skill for analytical reflection. One of the first acts of rebellion that anticipates Edna's sexual awakening is her refusal to obey her husband's command that she go inside the house after dark. Instead, she swings in the hammock until the moon sets. Resisting the confinement of the enclosed domestic space, she is unshielded from the chthonic mysteries of the moon and the terrors of the night associated with the primordial female realm.

Many readers interpret Edna's move from her husband's large house into a cottage of her own as an indication of growth, but it can also be understood as regression and retreat. In many respects, her new home, her "pigeon house" as she calls it, is just a smaller cage. A pigeon, after all, is a domesticated dove. Madame Reisz tells her that the "bird that would soar above the level plain of tradition and prejudice must have strong wings" (Chap. 27). But the novel is filled with images of birds with broken wings, lame birds that cannot fly. Edna's limited ability to direct her energy and to master her emotions is symbolized by her desire to learn to swim "far out where no woman had swum before." Her newly acquired aquatic skills are illusory: "A feeling of exultation overtook her, as if some power of significant import had been *given her* to control the working of her body and soul. She grew daring and reckless, overestimating her strength" [italics mine]. As indicated by the passive verb construction, Edna never gains the stamina that would enable her to stay above the waves for a long time, to resist the current or to swim against the tide. The same passivity and lack of commitment are evident in her efforts to paint: "When the weather was dark and cloudy, Edna could not work. She needed the sun to mellow and temper her mood to the sticking point" (Chap. 25). The sun, traditional symbol of male power, remains the driving force of her life. Like the moon, she lacks the ability to generate her own light or energy.

Ambition, striving, overcoming odds, the focusing of energy on a goal are habits of mind associated with masculine mastery. A woman who wants to develop these skills has to defy a centuries-old tradition of passive femininity. She has to possess the "courageous soul" as Madame Reisz tells her, "The brave soul. The soul that dares and defies" (Chap. 21). But Edna Pontellier does not have the emotional resources to transcend the conventions that regulate female behavior, conventions that she has, in fact, internalized. As we have seen, although Edna has freed herself from the domestic imperatives of her husband's house, she becomes ensnared by romantic love, which, masquerading as freedom, actually undercuts her possibility of autonomy. Her love for Robert consists of agonized longing and unrequited sexual need and seems to be a masochistic exercise in negative capability.

Lacking a tradition of self-assertion to guide her, Edna internalizes her anger, experiencing it as overwhelming depression: "Despondency had come upon her in the wakeful night, and had never lifted" (Chap. 39). Even her suicide is not willed. She returns to Grand Isle, and in a Whitmanesque moment, she stands by the sea "absolutely alone . . . for the first time in her life she stood naked in the air, at the mercy of the sun, the breeze that beat upon her, and the waves that invited her" (Chap. 39). But Whitman's scenario does not work for Edna: The sun, the water, and the air are active agents, and Edna is passive. Although she feels "new born," the diction foreshadows her destruction: "The foamy wavelets curled up to her white feet, and coiled like serpents around her ankles" (Chap. 39). As though she has no volition, she is drawn into the sea which is "sensuous, enfolding the body in its close embrace." As she swims away from the shore, the distinction between present and past is blurred for Edna, who is immersed in process, movement without purpose. Hopelessly tangled in a web of cultural constraints and biological necessity, she is impelled to escape her binding domesticity: "She thought of Leonce and the children. They were part of her life. But they need not have thought that they could possess her, body and soul" (Chap. 39). Perhaps her suicide can be interpreted as an act of angry defiance, but it is important to understand that it is an act without will: "Exhaustion was pressing upon and overpowering her . . . the shore was far behind her, and her strength was gone" (Chap. 39). Edna sinks into death, just as she drifts in life.

It is extremely important to note that Edna's last words – "Good-bye – *because* I love you" [italics mine] – contain the coded message that neither the domestic nor the romantic tradition can sustain the new woman. As Nina Baym points out, "But one important thought in Edna's mind when she walks into the sea is her inability to reconcile any possible independent existence with the lives of her children."[52] Either she is ensnared in the web of biological necessity and the concomitant bourgeois imperatives, or she is buffeted by the storms of romantic passion without the possibility of a social mooring; Edna knows that her erotic longing for Robert is another form of enslavement. Both the bourgeois code and the ideal of romantic possibility have failed her.

As we have seen, *The Awakening* ricochets between the poles of realism and romance. The novel has its origins in the American literary tradition of the conversion narrative, which has formed the basis for individual and social change from the diaries of Cotton Mather and Samuel Sewall through the journals of Thoreau and Emerson. After her awakening into a new sense of selfhood at Caminda Chenière (sunny isle), Edna disengages from domestic identity. This separation process is an essential aspect of the dynamic of protest and reform that is characteristic of American social change. Interestingly, it is the romantic quest, a secularized form of religious mission, that creates the means for Edna's personal transformation. A concomitant of Edna's erotic attraction to Robert is that she becomes increasingly aware of her personal preferences. During the time she is waiting for Robert to return from Mexico, she begins to paint seriously. On one level, the novel presents the iconography of romance in the most trite form – love letters, moonlight walks, island journeys – but on another level, the romantic mode is depicted as having a subversive function. As the novel makes clear, passion destabilizes and decenters the established social structure. The bourgeois order represented by the elaborate domestic rituals of the Pontellier household is seriously weakened by Edna's defection, so much so that her husband acts swiftly to conceal the upheaval by deciding to remodel the house.

Individualism and domesticity have coexisted in an uneasy alliance in the American household since the time of the Puritans. The Puritans made it illegal for people to live alone and described living outside a family as "living for oneself." This tension between self-development and family harmony, traditionally mediated by ritualized responsibilities and separate spheres of activity, became especially acute during the second half of the eighteenth century, when the ethos of individual liberty in the form of laissez-faire capitalism and Jacksonian/Emersonian individualism was contradicted by the idealization of the "lady" or "true woman,"

24

which, in fact, was a cultural representation of the confinement of female energy. The "true woman" was a social construction that prevented women from participating in the larger social processes – most notably politics. Refinement, sensibility, and prudence functioned to contain unruly impulses euphemistically described as "enthusiasm." Internalized censorship dictated by the feminine ethos prevented unpredictable female sexual energy from disrupting the tranquility of the home. In the opening paragraphs of *The Awakening*, domesticity is symbolized by the ornamental caged parrot, whose wildness has been tamed for the amusement of the household, and the mockingbird, whose contrapuntal imitations provide an ironic commentary on the activities of the kitchen. It is noteworthy that Leonce Pontellier is described as having the privilege of "quitting their society when they ceased to be entertaining." As we have seen, Edna breaks the mold of feminine refinement; her large frame and gestures overpower the diminished scale on which a lady lives. Her body is described as noble, not delicate; her movements are large and expressive, her appetites robust. She is not a "mother-woman," nor is she a woman warrior. Instead, as her name suggests, she is "one who bridges" – Pontellier – the traditional affiliative, instrumental, feminine mode and the aggressive, autonomous ideals of the new woman.

The essays in this volume are far-ranging indeed, and their diversity suggests that the richness and complexity of *The Awakening* endures. In her essay, "Tradition and the Female Talent: *The Awakening* as a Solitary Book," Elaine Showalter places Chopin's novel in the "transitional phase of woman's writing" – that is, after the period of the 1850s and 1860s, when Harriet Beecher Stowe, Susan Warner, E. D. E. N. Southworth, and the post–Civil War novelists like Louisa May Alcott and Elizabeth Stuart Phelps flourished, but before the modernist period in which the new woman writer found her full voice. Although Chopin rejects the material of the domestic novel, which upholds marriage and motherhood (as a focus of the female life cycle), she nevertheless resorts to the traditional resolution of the rebellious heroine's conflicts – self-destruction. As Showalter points out, drowning is a frequent "fictional punishment for female transgression." Showalter also observes that Madame Ratignolle and Mademoiselle Reisz "represent important alternatives and influences for Edna [and] . . . suggest different plots and conclusions." Adele Ratignolle, as the true woman, represents traditional conclusions to the sentimental plot, namely, a retreat into domesticity, whereas Mademoiselle Reisz holds up the ideal of surviving the harsh endurance test that is the inevitable fate of the unconventional spirit. Identified with the masculine romantic ideal that the creative person can find no home in the conventional world, Mademoiselle Reisz retreats into a solitary existence that is sometimes as confining as the web of domesticity. Showalter argues that although Chopin "wished to reject both of these endings – the domestic and the romantic – and to escape from the literary traditions they represent, the author of *The Awakening* was unable to create a new plot or formulation of women's lives."

Michael T. Gilmore's essay, "Revolt Against Nature: The Problematic Modernism of *The Awakening*," demonstrates the ways in which Chopin's novel is a premodernist effort to debunk the ideals – social and aesthetic – of her culture. Not only does Edna's "revolt against the family also constitute a threat to property," her rebellion "calls civilization into question." For Gilmore, Edna's suicide is not a capitulation but an act of rebellion against her claustrophobic world. Nothing less than a "transformation of social reality would enable the 'new born' creature Edna has become to go on living."

Gilmore sees Chopin as a pioneer of the "self-referential" modernist agenda and *The Awakening* as presenting a "series of challenges to the ideology of representation" characteristic of traditional realism. By situating the novel in "subversive relation to the mimetic idea," Chopin creates a work in which poetic expressiveness conveys the subjectivity necessary for the creation of alternate visions. As both Gilmore and Showalter point out, Chopin's novel uses considerably more dream and fantasy material than the work of her predecessors. This emphasis on the subjective is a prelude to the decentering of the self in relation to experience – a decentering that is essential to modernism. As part of the tradition of the new woman writer, Chopin rejects the notion of immutable natural laws that regulate family and society; instead, she subscribes to the belief in individual autonomy and freedom of choice.

In a much more conservative essay, "The Half-Life of Edna Pontellier," Andrew Delbanco notes that the novel is concerned with "suspension not merely between Kentucky Presbyterianism and Creole Catholicism, nor between halves of the city as divided by Canal Street, but between the genders themselves." Observing that Edna Pontellier struggles to define an "essential self" in this culture of bifurcations, Delbanco argues that she fails to do so because she ultimately succumbs to the love of power that is "no less corrosive to her character than it is to her husband's." *The Awakening,* then, according to Delbanco, is a novel of "passing" — that is, it is "about a woman passing for a man." Arguing that Chopin does not provide an alternative to either submission to or emulation of male power, Delbanco sees Edna as capitulating to the numbing masculine world of laissez-faire individualism and "commodity-display" exchange.

In "Edna's Wisdom: A Transitional and Numinous Merging," Cristina Giorcelli observes that Edna represents liminal consciousness; that is, Edna's awareness focuses on the threshold of perception rather than on clearly bounded and demarcated experience. The liminal state is characterized by ambiguity and complexity; although this psychological indeterminacy sometimes borders on incoherence or chaos, it also creates a sense of possibility, of new beginnings and new social scenarios. In the "in-between" status between the world of women and the world of men, between night and day, emotion and reason, purpose and diffusion, Edna exists in a dynamic, mutable, labyrinthine world. According to Giorcelli, Edna's life represents the endless cycle of birth and death, but also holds forth the possibility that she can "bridge distances" and "mitigate polarities." And Giorcelli also sees Edna as an archetypal embodiment of the Persephone–Artemis–Athene triad that suggests the mother, daughter, and virgin aspects of femininity. In her multiple roles, Edna explores female possibility from which the woman of the future will be born. In a process not unlike that of a reverse Venus emerging from the sea, Edna merges with the undifferentiated female element almost as if in an effort to surface in another point of the female life cycle. Of course, Giorcelli's optimistic interpretation emphasizes the metaphoric rather than the literal dimension of the text. While it is true that ontological flux is the harbinger of possibility, the physical fact of Edna's death cannot be interpreted solely as a trope.

The essays in this book suggest but a few of the extraordinary range of possible interpretations of *The Awakening*. In addition to presenting the tensions and conflicts in the life of the emerging new woman in the late nineteenth and early twentieth centuries in American culture, Kate Chopin created an evocative portrait of Edna Pontellier as the woman whose life bridges two traditions — domestic femininity and romantic individualism — and whose death reminds us not only of human limitation but also of human possibility. It is ironic that Edna Pontellier sacrifices her life for the ideal of personal freedom; nevertheless, her suicide indicates that personal autonomy is not an ineffable ideal but a priority that is deeply embedded in American life.

NOTES

1. Felix Chopin, *St. Louis Post-Dispatch,* November 26, 1899, p. 6.
2. Per Seyersted, *Kate Chopin: A Critical Biography* (New York: Octagon Books, 1980), pp. 31–2. I am indebted to this study for biographical information on Kate Chopin.
3. Daniel S. Rankin, *Kate Chopin and Her Creole Stories* (Philadelphia: University of Pennsylvania Press, 1932), p. 35.
4. Per Seyersted, ed., *The Complete Works of Kate Chopin* (Baton Rouge: Louisiana State University Press, 1969), pp. 700–1.
5. *Sunday Mirror,* 4 (April 15, 1894); 4; *Sunday Mirror,* 4 (September 30, 1894), 4; *Atlantic Monthly* 73 (April 1894), 558–9.
6. Seyersted, *Complete Works,* pp. 352–4.
7. Seyersted, *Kate Chopin,* pp. 58–9.
8. Frances Porcher, "Kate Chopin's Novel," *The Mirror,* 9 (May 4, 1899), 6.
9. Anon., "Book Reviews," *Public Opinion,* 26 (June 22, 1899), 794.
10. Anon., "Fiction," *Literature* 4 (June 23, 1899), 570.
11. Anon., "Books of the Week," *Providence Sunday Journal* (June 4, 1899), 15.

12. Anon., "Fresh Literature," *Los Angeles Sunday Times* (June 25, 1899), 12.

13. Anon., "Notes from Bookland," *St. Louis Daily Globe-Democrat* (May 13, 1899), 5.

14. C. L. Deyo, "The Newest Books," *St. Louis Post-Dispatch* (May 20, 1899), 4.

15. Anon., "Books of the Day," *Chicago Times-Herald* (June 1, 1899), 9.

16. Anon., "New Publications," *New Orleans Times-Democrat* (June 18, 1899), 15.

17. Sibert [Willa Cather], "Books and Magazines," *Pittsburgh Leader* (July 8, 1899), 6.

18. Quoted in Rankin, *Kate Chopin*, p. 173.

19. Kate Chopin, "Aims and Autographs of Authors," *Book News* 17 (July 1899), 612.

20. Kate Chopin papers, Missouri Historical Society, quoted in Per Seyersted and Emily Toth, eds., *A Kate Chopin Miscellany* (Natchitoches, La.: The Northwestern State University Press, 1979), p. 143.

21. Kate Chopin, "Reflection," quoted in Seyersted, *Kate Chopin*, p. 181.

22. Seyersted, *Kate Chopin*, p. 198.

23. Ibid., p. 180.

24. F. L. Patee, *The Development of the American Short Story*, (New York: Harper & Brothers, 1923), pp. 324–7.

25. Dorothy Ann Dondore, "Kate O'Flaherty Chopin," *Dictionary of American Biography*, Vol. IV (New York: Scribner's, 1930), pp. 90–1.

26. Rankin, *Kate Chopin*, p. 140.

27. Arthur Hobson Quinn, *American Fiction* (New York: Appleton-Century, 1936), pp. 354–7.

28. Carlos Baker, "Delineation of Life and Character," in Robert E. Spiller, ed., *Literary History of the United States*, Vol. I (New York: Macmillan, 1948), pp. 858–9.

29. Cyrille Arnavon, "Les Débuts du Roman Réaliste Américain et l' Influence Française" in Henri Kerst, ed., *Romanciers Américain Contemporains* (Paris: Librairie Didier, 1946), pp. 9–35.

30. Clarence Gohdes, "Exploitation of the Provinces," in Arthur Hobson Quinn, ed., *The Literature of the American People* (New York: Appleton-Century-Crofts, 1951), p. 654; Van Wyck Brooks, *The Confident Years: 1885–1915*, (New York: Dutton, 1952), p. 241.

31. Edmund Wilson, *Patriotic Gore* (New York: Oxford University Press, 1962), pp. 587–93.

32. Larzar Ziff, *The American 1890's: Life and Times of a Lost Generation* (New York: Viking Press, 1966), p. 305.

33. Kenneth Eble, "A Forgotten Novel: Kate Chopin's *The Awakening*," *Western Humanities Review* 10 (Summer 1956):269. Per Seyersted, *Kate Chopin*, p. 196.

34. Lewis Leary, *Southern Excursions: Essays on Mark Twain and Others* (Baton Rouge: Louisiana State University Press, 1971), p. 169.

35. Jules Chametzky, "Our Decentralized Literature," *Jahrbuch fur Amerikastudien* (1972):72. Donald A. Ringe, "Romantic Imagery in Kate Chopin's *The Awakening*," *American Literature* 43 (January 1972): 588.

36. George Arms, "Kate Chopin's *The Awakening* in the Perspective of Her Literary Career," in Clarence Gohdes, ed., *Essays on American Literature in Honor of Jay B. Hubbell,* (Durham: Duke University Press, 1967), pp. 215–28.

37. George M. Spangler, "Kate Chopin's *The Awakening:* A Partial Dissent," *Novel* 3 (Spring 1970):249–55.

38. Cynthia Griffin Wolff, "Thanatos and Eros: Kate Chopin's *The Awakening*," *American Quarterly* 5 (October 1973):449–71.

39. Ringe, "Romantic Imagery," 588.

40. Ruth Sullivan and Stewart Smith, "Narrative Stance in Kate Chopin's *The Awakening*," *Studies in American Fiction* 1 (Spring 1973):62–75. Kenneth M. Rosen, "Kate Chopin's *The Awakening:* Ambiguity as Art," *Journal of American Studies* 5 (August 1971):197–200.

41. Suzanne Wolkenfield, "Edna's Suicide: The Problem of the One and the Many," in Margaret Culley, ed., *The Awakening* (New York: Norton, 1976), pp. 218–24. In the same volume, see also Margaret Culley, "Edna Pontellier: 'A Solitary Soul,'" pp. 224–8.

42. Culley, "Edna Pontellier," pp. 224–8.

43. Theodore Dreiser, *Sister Carrie* (New York: Doubleday, Page, 1900), p. 353.

44. Mary L. Shaffter, "Creole Women," *The Chautauquan* 15 (June 1892):346–7. Reprinted in Culley, *The Awakening,* pp. 119–21.

45. Culley, *The Awakening,* p. 118.

46. Wilbur Fisk Tillet, "Southern Womanhood as Affected by the Civil War," *The Century Magazine* 43 (November 1891):16. See also Anne Firor Scott, *The Southern Lady: From Pedestal to Politics, 1830–1930* (Chicago: The University of Chicago Press, 1970).

47. Culley, *The Awakening,* p. 135.

48. Ibid.

49. Sandra Gilbert, Introduction to *The Awakening* (New York: Penguin Books, 1985), p. 31.
50. Nina Baym, Introduction to *The Awakening* (New York, Modern Library, 1981), p. xxxviii.
51. Seyersted, *Kate Chopin*, pp. 147, 221.
52. Baym, Introduction to *The Awakening*, p. xxxvii.

Tradition and the Female Talent:
The Awakening as a Solitary Book

ELAINE SHOWALTER

"WHATEVER we may do or attempt, despite the embrace and transports of love, the hunger of the lips, we are always alone. I have dragged you out into the night in the vain hope of a moment's escape from the horrible solitude which overpowers me. But what is the use! I speak and you answer me, and still each of us is alone; side by side but alone."[1] In 1895, these words, from a story by Guy de Maupassant called "Solitude," which she had translated for a St. Louis magazine, expressed an urbane and melancholy wisdom that Kate Chopin found compelling. To a woman who had survived the illusions that friendship, romance, marriage, or even motherhood would provide lifelong companionship and identity, and who had come to recognize the existential solitude of all human beings, Maupassant's declaration became a kind of credo. Indeed, *The Awakening*, which Chopin subtitled "A Solitary Soul," may be read as an account of Edna Pontellier's evolution from romantic fantasies of fusion with another person to self-definition and self-reliance. At the beginning of the novel, in the midst of the bustling social world of Grand Isle, caught in her domestic roles of wife and mother, Edna pictures solitude as alien, masculine, and frightening, a naked man standing beside a "desolate rock" by the sea in an attitude of "hopeless resignation" (Chap. 9). By the end, she has claimed a solitude that is defiantly feminine, returning to the nearly empty island off-season, to stand naked and "absolutely alone" by the shore and to elude "the soul's slavery" by plunging into the sea's embrace (Chap. 39).

Yet Edna's triumphant embrace of solitude could not be the choice of Kate Chopin as an artist. A writer may work in solitude, but literature depends on a tradition, on shared forms and representations of experience; and literary genres, like biological species, evolve because of significant innovations by individuals that survive through imitation and revision. Thus it can be a very serious blow to a developing genre when a revolutionary work is taken out of circulation. Experimentation is retarded and repressed, and it may be several generations before the evolution of the literary genre catches up. The interruption of this evolutionary process is most destructive for the literature of a minority group, in which writers have to contend with cultural prejudices against their creative gifts. Yet radical departures from literary convention within a minority tradition are especially likely to be censured and suppressed by the dominant culture, because they violate social as well as aesthetic stereotypes and expectations.

The Awakening was just such a revolutionary book. Generally recognized today as the first aesthetically successful novel to have been written by an American woman, it marked a significant epoch in the evolution of an American female literary tradition. As an American woman novelist of the 1890s, Kate Chopin had inherited a rich and complex tradition, composed not only of her American female precursors but also of American transcendentalism, European realism, and *fin-de-siècle* feminism and aestheticism. In this context, *The Awakening* broke new thematic and stylistic ground. Chopin went boldly beyond the work of her precursors in writing about women's longing for sexual and personal emancipation.

Yet the novel represents a literary beginning as abruptly cut off as its heroine's awakening consciousness. Edna Pontellier's explicit violations of the modes and codes of nineteenth-century American women's behavior shocked contemporary critics, who described *The Awakening* as "morbid," "essentially vulgar," and "gilded dirt."[2] Banned in Kate Chopin's own city of St. Louis and censured in the national press, *The Awakening* thus became a solitary book, one that dropped out of sight, and that remained unsung by literary historians and unread by several generations of American women writers.

In many respects, *The Awakening* seems to comment on its own history as a novel, to predict its own critical fate. The parallels between the experiences of Edna Pontellier, as she breaks away

34

from the conventional feminine roles of wife and mother, and Kate Chopin, as she breaks away from conventions of literary domesticity, suggest that Edna's story may also be read as a parable of Chopin's literary awakening. Both the author and the heroine seem to be oscillating between two worlds, caught between contradictory definitions of femininity and creativity, and seeking either to synthesize them or to go beyond them to an emancipated womanhood and an emancipated fiction. Edna Pontellier's "unfocused yearning" for an autonomous life is akin to Kate Chopin's yearning to write works that go beyond female plots and feminine endings.

In the early stages of her career, Chopin had tried to follow the literary advice and literary examples of others and had learned that such dutiful efforts led only to imaginative stagnation. By the late 1890s, when she wrote *The Awakening,* Chopin had come to believe that the true artist was one who defied tradition, who rejected both the "convenances" of respectable morality and the conventions and formulas of literary success. What impressed her most about Maupassant was that he had "escaped from tradition and authority . . . had entered into himself and looked out upon life through his own being and with his own eyes."[3] This is very close to what happens to Edna Pontellier as she frees herself from social obligations and received opinions and begins "to look with her own eyes; to see and to apprehend the deeper undercurrents of life" (Chap. 32). Much as she admired Maupassant, and much as she learned from translating his work, Chopin felt no desire to imitate him. Her sense of the need for independence and individuality in writing is dramatically expressed in *The Awakening* by Mademoiselle Reisz, who tells Edna that the artist must possess "the courageous soul that dares and defies" (Chap. 21) and must have strong wings to soar "above the level plain of tradition and prejudice" (Chap. 27).

Nonetheless, in order to understand *The Awakening* fully, we need to read it in the context of literary tradition. Even in its defiant solitude, *The Awakening* speaks for a transitional phase in American women's writing, and Chopin herself would never have written the books she did without a tradition to admire and oppose. When she wrote *The Awakening* in 1899, Chopin could look back to at least two generations of female literary precursors. The antebellum novelists, led by Harriet Beecher Stowe, Susan Warner, and E. D. E. N. Southworth, were the first members of these generations. Born in the early decades of the nineteenth century, they began to publish stories and novels in the 1850s and 1860s that reflected the dominant expressive and symbolic models of an American woman's culture. The historian Carroll Smith-Rosenberg has called this culture the "female world of love and ritual," and it was primarily defined by the veneration of motherhood, by intense mother–daughter bonds, and by intimate female friendships. As Smith-Rosenberg explains: "Uniquely female rituals drew women together during every stage of their lives, from adolescence through courtship, marriage, childbirth and child rearing, death and mourning. Women revealed their deepest feelings to one another, helped one another with the burdens of housewifery and motherhood, nursed one another's sick, and mourned for one another's dead."[4] Although premarital relationships between the sexes were subject to severe restrictions, romantic friendships between women were admired and encouraged. The nineteenth-century ideal of female "passionlessness" – the belief that women did not have the same sexual desires as men – had advantages as well as disadvantages for women. It reinforced the notion that women were the purer and more spiritual sex, and thus were morally superior to men. Furthermore, as the historian Nancy F. Cott has argued, "acceptance of the idea of passionlessness created sexual solidarity among women; it allowed women to consider their love relationships with one another of higher character than heterosexual relationships because they excluded (male) carnal passion."[5] "I do not believe that men can ever feel so pure an enthusiasm for women as we can feel for one another," wrote the novelist Catherine Sedgwick. "Ours is nearest to the love of angels."[6] The homosocial world of women's culture in fact allowed much leeway for physical intimacy and touch; "girls routinely slept together, kissed and hugged one another."[7] But these caresses were not interpreted as erotic expressions.

The mid-nineteenth-century code of values growing out of women's culture, which Mary Ryan calls "the empire of the mother," was also sustained by sermons, child-rearing manuals, and

sentimental fiction.[8] Women writers advocated motherly influence – "gentle nurture," "sweet control," and "educating power"
– as an effective solution to such social problems as alcoholism,
crime, slavery, and war. As Harriet Beecher Stowe proclaimed,
"The 'Woman Question' of the day is: Shall MOTHERHOOD ever
be felt in the public administration of the affairs of state?"[9]

As writers, however, the sentimentalists looked to motherhood
for their metaphors and justifications of literary creativity. "Creating a story is like bearing a child," wrote Stowe, "and it leaves me
in as weak and helpless a state as when my baby was born."[10]
Thematically and stylistically, pre–Civil War women's fiction,
variously described as "literary domesticity" or the "sentimental
novel," celebrates matriarchal institutions and idealizes the period
of blissful bonding between mother and child. It is permeated by
the artifacts, spaces, and images of nineteenth-century American
domestic culture: the kitchen, with its worn rocking chair; the
Edenic mother's garden, with its fragrant female flowers and ener-
getic male bees; the caged songbird, which represents the creative
woman in her domestic sphere. Women's narratives were formally
composed of brief sketches joined together like the pieces of a
patchwork quilt; they frequently alluded to specific quilt patterns
and followed quilt design conventions of repetition, variation, and
contrast. Finally, their most intense representation of female sexual pleasure was not in terms of heterosexual romance, but rather
the holding or suckling of a baby; for, as Mary Ryan points out,
"nursing an infant was one of the most hallowed and inviolate
episodes in a woman's life. . . . Breast-feeding was sanctioned as
'one of the most important duties of female life,' 'one of peculiar,
inexpressible felicity,' and 'the sole occupation and pleasure' of a
new mother."[11]

The cumulative effect of all these covert appeals to female solidarity in books written by, for, and about women could be a
subversive critique of patriarchal power. Yet aesthetically the fiction of this generation was severely restricted. The sentimentalists
did not identify with the figure of the "artist," the "genius," or the
"poet" promulgated by patriarchal culture. As Nina Baym explains, "they conceptualized authorship as a profession rather
than a calling. . . . Women authors tended not to think of them-

37

selves as artists or justify themselves in the language of art until the 1870s and after."[12] In the writing of the sentimentalists, "the dimensions of formal self-consciousness, attachment to or quarrel with a grand tradition, aesthetic seriousness, are all missing. Often the women deliberately and even proudly disavowed membership in an artistic fraternity."[13] Insofar as art implied a male club or circle of brothers, women felt excluded from it. Instead they claimed affiliation with a literary sorority, a society of sisters whose motives were moral rather than aesthetic, whose ambitions were to teach and to influence rather than to create. Although their books sold by the millions, they were not taken seriously by male critics.

The next generation of American women writers, however, found themselves in a different cultural situation. After the Civil War, the homosocial world of women's culture began to dissolve as women demanded entrance to higher education, the professions, and the political world. The female local colorists who began to publish stories about American regional life in the 1870s and 1880s were also attracted to the male worlds of art and prestige opening up to women, and they began to assert themselves as the daughters of literary fathers as well as literary mothers. Claiming both male and female aesthetic models, they felt free to present themselves as artists and to write confidently about the art of fiction in such essays as Elizabeth Stuart Phelps's "Art for Truth's Sake".[14] Among the differences the local colorists saw between themselves and their predecessors was the question of "selfishness," the ability to put literary ambitions before domestic duties. Although she had been strongly influenced in her work by Harriet Beecher Stowe's *Pearl of Orr's Island*, Sarah Orne Jewett came to believe that Stowe's work was "incomplete" because she was unable to "bring herself to that cold selfishness of the moment for one's work's sake."[15]

Writers of this generation chose to put their work first. The 1870s and 1880s were what Susan B. Anthony called "an epoch of single women,"[16] and many unmarried women writers of this generation lived alone; others were involved in "Boston marriages," or long-term relationships with another woman. But despite their individual lifestyles, many speculated in their writing on the conflicts between maternity and artistic creativity. Motherhood no longer seemed to be the motivating force of writing, but rather its opposite. Thus artistic fulfillment required the sacrifice of maternal drives, and maternal fulfillment meant giving up artistic ambitions.

The conflicts between love and work that Edna Pontellier faces in *The Awakening* were anticipated in such earlier novels as Louisa May Alcott's unfinished *Diana and Persis* (1879) and Elizabeth Stuart Phelps's *The Story of Avis* (1879). A gifted painter who has studied in Florence and Paris, Avis does not intend to marry. As she tells her suitor, "My ideals of art are those with which marriage is perfectly incompatible. Success – for a woman – means absolute surrender, in whatever direction. Whether she paints a picture, or loves a man, there is no division of labor possible in her economy. To the attainment of any end worth living for, a symmetrical sacrifice of her nature is compulsory upon her." But love persuades her to change her mind, and the novel records the inexorable destruction of her artistic genius as domestic responsibilities, maternal cares, and her husband's failures use up her energy. By the end of the novel, Avis has become resigned to the idea that her life is a sacrifice for the next generation of women. Thinking back to her mother, a talented actress who gave up her profession to marry and died young, and looking at her daughter, Wait, Avis takes heart in the hope that it may take three generations to create the woman who can unite "her supreme capacity of love" with the "sacred individuality of her life."[17] As women's culture declined after the Civil War, moreover, the local colorists mourned its demise by investing its traditional images with mythic significance. In their stories, the mother's garden has become a paradisal sanctuary; the caged bird a wild white heron, or heroine of nature; the house an emblem of the female body, with the kitchen as its womb; and the artifacts of domesticity virtually totemic objects. In Jewett's *Country of the Pointed Firs*, for example, the braided rag rug has become a kind of prayer mat of concentric circles from which the matriarchal priestess, Mrs. Todd, delivers her sybilline pronouncements. The woman artist in this fiction expresses her conflicting needs most fully in her quasi-religious dedication to these artifacts of a bygone age.

The New Women writers of the 1890s no longer grieved for the female bonds and sanctuaries of the past. Products of both Darwinian skepticism and aesthetic sophistication, they had an ambivalent or even hostile relationship to women's culture, which they often saw as boring and restrictive. Their attitudes toward female sexuality were also revolutionary. A few radical feminists had always maintained that women's sexual apathy was not an innately feminine attribute but rather the result of prudery and repression; some women's rights activitists too had privately confessed that, as Elizabeth Cady Stanton wrote in her diary in 1883, "a healthy woman has as much passion as a man."[18] Not all New Women advocated female sexual emancipation; the most zealous advocates of free love were male novelists such as Grant Allen, whose best-seller, *The Woman Who Did* (1895), became a byword of the decade. But the heroine of ɪTew Woman fiction, as Linda Dowling has explained, "expressed her quarrel with Victorian culture chiefly through sexual means – by heightening sexual consciousness, candor, and expression."[19] No wonder, then, that reviewers saw *The Awakening* as part of the "overworked field of sex fiction" or noted that since "San Francisco and Paris, and London, and New York had furnished Women Who Did, why not New Orleans?"[20]

In the form as well as the content of their work, New Women writers demanded freedom and innovation. They modified the realistic three-decker novels about courtship and marriage that had formed the bulk of midcentury "woman's fiction" to make room for interludes of fantasy and parable, especially episodes "in which a woman will dream of an entirely different world or will cross-dress, experimenting with the freedom available to boys and men."[21] Instead of the crisply plotted short stories that had been the primary genre of the local colorists, writers such as Olive Schreiner, Ella D'Arcy, Sarah Grand, and "George Egerton" (Mary Chavelita Dunne) experimented with new fictional forms that they called "keynotes," "allegories," "fantasies," "monochromes," or "dreams." As Egerton explained, these impressionistic narratives were efforts to explore a hitherto unrecorded female consciousness: "I realized that in literature everything had been done better by man than woman could hope to emulate. There was only one small plot left for herself to tell: the *terra incognita* of herself, as she knew herself to be, not as man liked to imagine her – in a word to give herself away, as man had given himself away in his writings."[22]

Kate Chopin's literary evolution took her progressively through the three phases of nineteenth-century American women's culture and women's writing. Born in 1850, she grew up with the great best-sellers of the American and English sentimentalists. As a girl, she had wept over the works of Warner and Stowe and had copied pious passages from the English novelist Dinah Mulock Craik's *The Woman's Kingdom* into her diary. Throughout her adolescence, Chopin had also shared an intimate friendship with Kitty Garasché, a classmate at the Academy of the Sacred Heart. Together, Chopin recalled, the girls had read fiction and poetry, gone on excursions, and "exchanged our heart secrets."[23] Their friendship ended in 1870 when Kate Chopin married and Kitty Garasché entered a convent. Yet when Oscar Chopin died in 1883, his young widow went to visit her old friend and was shocked by her blind isolation from the world. When Chopin began to write, she took as her models such local colorists as Sarah Orne Jewett and Mary Wilkins Freeman, who had not only mastered technique and construction but had also devoted themselves to telling the stories of female loneliness, isolation, and frustration.

Sandra Gilbert has suggested that local color was a narrative strategy that Chopin employed to solve a specific problem: how to deal with extreme psychological states without the excesses of sentimental narrative and without critical recrimination. At first, Gilbert suggests, "local color" writing "offered both a mode and a manner that could mediate between the literary structures she had inherited and those she had begun." Like the anthropologist, the local colorist could observe vagaries of culture and character with "almost scientific detachment." Furthermore, "by reporting odd events and customs that were part of a region's 'local color' she could tell what would ordinarily be rather shocking or even melodramatic tales in an unmelodramatic way, and without fear of . . . moral outrage."[24]

But before long, Chopin looked beyond the oddities of the local colorists to more ambitious models. Her literary tastes were anything but parochial. She read widely in a variety of genres — Darwin, Spencer, and Huxley, as well as Aristophanes, Flaubert, Whitman, Swinburne, and Ibsen. In particular, she associated her own literary and psychological awakening with Maupassant. "Here was life, not fiction," she wrote of his influence on her, "for where were the plots, the old fashioned mechanism and stage trapping that in a vague, unthinking way I had fancied were essential to the art of story making."[25] In a review of a book by the local colorist Hamlin Garland, Chopin expressed her dissatisfaction with the restricted subjects of regional writing: "Social problems, social environments, local color, and the rest of it" could not "insure the survival of a writer who employs them."[26] She resented being compared to George Washington Cable or Grace King.[27] Furthermore, she did not share the female local colorists' obsession with the past, their desperate nostalgia for a bygone idealized age. "How curiously the past effaces itself for me!" she wrote in her diary in 1894. "I cannot live through yesterday or tomorrow."[28] Unlike Jewett, Freeman, King, or Woolson, she did not favor the old woman as narrator.

Despite her identification with the New Women, however, Chopin was not an activist. She never joined the women's suffrage movement or belonged to a female literary community. Indeed, her celebrated St. Louis literary salon attracted mostly male journalists, editors, and writers. Chopin resigned after only two years from a St. Louis women's literary and charitable society. When her children identified her close friends to be interviewed by her first biographer, Daniel Rankin, there were no women on the list.[29]

Thus Chopin certainly did not wish to write a didactic feminist novel. In reviews published in the 1890s, she indicated her impatience with novelists such as Zola and Hardy, who tried to instruct their readers. She distrusted the rhetoric of such feminist bestsellers as Sarah Grand's *The Heavenly Twins* (1893). The eleventh commandment, she noted, is "Thou shalt not preach."[30] Instead she would try to record, in her own way and in her own voice, the *terra incognita* of a woman's "inward life" in all its "vague, tangled, chaotic" tumult.

Much of the shock effect of *The Awakening* to the readers of 1899 came from Chopin's rejection of the conventions of women's writing. Despite her name, which echoes two famous heroines of the domestic novel (Edna Earl in Augusta Evans's *St. Elmo* and Edna Kenderdine in Dinah Craik's *The Woman's Kingdom*), Edna Pontellier appears to reject the domestic empire of the mother and the sororal world of women's culture. Seemingly beyond the bonds of womanhood, she has neither mother nor daughter, and even refuses to go to her sister's wedding.

Moreover, whereas the sentimental heroine nurtures others, and the abstemious local color heroine subsists upon meager vegetarian diets, Kate Chopin's heroine is a robust woman who does not deny her appetites. Freeman's New England nun picks at her dainty lunch of lettuce leaves and currants, but Edna Pontellier eats hearty meals of paté, pompano, steak, and broiled chicken; bites off chunks of crusty bread; snacks on beer and Gruyere cheese; and sips brandy, wine, and champagne.

Formally, too, the novel has moved away from conventional techniques of realism to an impressionistic rhythm of epiphany and mood. Chopin abandoned the chapter titles she had used in her first novel, *At Fault* (1890), for thirty-nine numbered chapters of uneven length, ranging from the single paragraph of Chapter 28 to the sustained narrative of the dinner party in Chapter 30. The chapters are unified less by their style than by their focus on Edna's consciousness, and by the repetition of key motifs and images: music, the sea, shadows, swimming, eating, sleeping, gambling, the lovers, birth. Chapters of lyricism and fantasy, such as Edna's voyage to the Chenière Caminada, alternate with realistic, even satirical, scenes of Edna's marriage.

Most important, where previous works ignored sexuality or spiritualized it through maternity, *The Awakening* is insistently sexual, explicitly involved with the body and with self-awareness through physical awareness. Although Edna's actual seduction by Arobin takes place in the narrative neverland between Chapters 31 and 32, Chopin brilliantly evokes sexuality through images and details. In keeping with the novel's emphasis on the self, several scenes suggest Edna's initial autoeroticism. Edna's midnight swim, which awakens the "first-felt throbbings of desire," takes place in an atmosphere of erotic fragrance, "strange, rare odors . . . a tangle of the sea-smell and of weeds and damp new-ploughed earth, mingled with the heavy perfume of a field of white blossoms" (Chap. 10). A similarly voluptuous scene is her nap at Chenière Caminada, when she examines her flesh as she lies in a "strange, quaint bed with its sweet country odor of laurel" (Chap. 13).

Edna reminds Dr. Mandelet of "some beautiful, sleek animal waking up in the sun" (Chap. 23), and we recall that among her fantasies in listening to music is the image of a lady stroking a cat. The image both conveys Edna's sensuality and hints at the self-contained, almost masturbatory, quality of her sexuality. Her rendezvous with Robert takes place in a sunny garden where both stroke a drowsy cat's silky fur, and Arobin first seduces her by smoothing her hair with his "soft, magnetic hand" (Chap. 31).

Yet despite these departures from tradition, there are other respects in which the novel seems very much of its time. As its title suggests, *The Awakening* is a novel about a process rather than a program, about a passage rather than a destination. Like Edith Wharton's *The House of Mirth* (1905), it is a transitional female fiction of the *fin-de-siècle,* a narrative of and about the passage from the homosocial women's culture and literature of the nineteenth century to the heterosexual fiction of modernism. Chopin might have taken the plot from a notebook entry Henry James made in 1892 about "the growing divorce between the American woman (with her comparative leisure, culture, grace, social instincts, artistic ambition) and the male American immersed in the ferocity of business, with no time for any but the most sordid interests, purely commercial, professional, democratic and political. This divorce is rapidly becoming a gulf."[31] The Gulf where the opening chapters of *The Awakening* are set certainly suggests the "growing divorce" between Edna's interests and desires and Leonce's obsessions with the stock market, property, and his brokerage business.

Yet in turning away from her marriage, Edna initially looks back to women's culture rather than forward to another man. As Sandra Gilbert has pointed out, Grand Isle is an oasis of women's culture, or a "female colony": "Madame Lebrun's pension on Grand Isle is very much a woman's land not only because it is owned and run by a single woman and dominated by 'mother-women' but also because (as in so many summer colonies today) its principal inhabitants are actually women and children whose husbands and fathers visit only on weekends . . . [and it is situated,] like so many places that are significant for women, outside patriarchal culture, beyond the limits and limitations of the city where men make history, on a shore that marks the margin where nature intersects with culture."[32]

Edna's awakening, moreover, begins not with a man, but with Adele Ratignolle, the empress of the "mother-women" of Grand Isle. A "self-contained" (Chap. 7) woman, Edna has never had any close relationships with members of her own sex. Thus it is Adele who belatedly initiates Edna into the world of female love and ritual on the first step of her sensual voyage of self-discovery. Edna's first attraction to Adele is physical: "the excessive physical charm of the Creole had first attracted her, for Edna had a sensuous susceptibility to beauty" (Chap. 7). At the beach, in the hot sun, she responds to Adele's caresses, the first she has ever known from another woman, as Adele clasps her hand "firmly and warmly" and strokes it fondly. The touch provokes Edna to an unaccustomed candor; leaning her head on Adele's shoulder and confiding some of her secrets, she begins to feel "intoxicated" (Chap. 7). The bond between them goes beyond sympathy, as Chopin notes, to "what we might well call love" (Chap. 7).

In some respects, the motherless Edna also seeks a mother surrogate in Adele and looks to her for nurturance. Adele provides maternal encouragement for Edna's painting and tells her that her "talent is immense" (Chap. 18). Characteristically, Adele has rationalized her own "art" as a maternal project: "she was keeping up her music on account of the children. . . a means of brightening the home and making it attractive" (Chap. 9). Edna's responses to Adele's music have been similarly tame and sentimental. Her revealing fantasies as she listens to Adele play her easy pieces suggest the restriction and decorum of the female world: "a dainty young woman . . . taking mincing dancing steps, as she came down a long avenue between tall hedges"; "children at play" (Chap. 9). Women's art, as Adele presents it, is social, pleasant, and undemanding. It does not conflict with her duties as a wife and mother, and can even be seen to enhance them. Edna understands this well; as she retorts when her husband recommends Adele as a model of an artist, "She isn't a musician and I'm not a painter!" (Chap. 19).

Yet the relationship with the conventional Adele educates the immature Edna to respond for the first time both to a different kind of sexuality and to the unconventional and difficult art of Mademoiselle Reisz. In responding to Adele's interest, Edna begins to think about her own past and to analyze her own personality. In textual terms, it is through this relationship that she becomes "Edna" in the narrative rather than "Mrs. Pontellier."

We see the next stage of Edna's awakening in her relationship with Mademoiselle Reisz, who initiates her into the world of art. Significantly, this passage also takes place through a female rather than a male mentor, and, as with Adele, there is something more intense than friendship between the two women. Whereas Adele's fondness for Edna, however, is depicted as maternal and womanly, Mademoiselle Reisz's attraction to Edna suggests something more perverse. The pianist is obsessed with Edna's beauty, raves over her figure in a bathing suit, greets her as "ma belle" and "ma reine," holds her hand, and describes herself as "a foolish old woman whom you have captivated" (Chap. 21). If Adele is a surrogate for Edna's dead mother and the intimate friend she never had as a girl, Mademoiselle Reisz, whose music reduces Edna to passionate sobs, seems to be a surrogate lover. And whereas Adele is a "faultless madonna" who speaks for the values and laws of the Creole community, Mademoiselle Reisz is a renegade, self-assertive and outspoken. She has no patience with petty social rules and violates the most basic expectations of femininity. To a rake like Arobin, she is so unattractive, unpleasant, and unwomanly as to seem "partially demented" (Chap. 27). Even Edna occasionally perceives Mademoiselle Reisz's awkwardness as a kind of deformity, and is sometimes offended by the old woman's candor and is not sure whether she likes her.

Yet despite her eccentricities, Mademoiselle Reisz seems "to reach Edna's spirit and set it free" (Chap. 26). Her voice in the novel seems to speak for the author's view of art and for the artist. It is surely no accident, for example, that it is Chopin's music that Mademoiselle Reisz performs. At the *pension* on Grand Isle, the pianist first plays a Chopin prelude, to which Edna responds with surprising turbulence: "the very passions themselves were aroused within her soul, swaying it, lashing it, as the waves daily beat upon her splendid body. She trembled, she was choking, and the tears blinded her" (Chap. 9). "Chopin" becomes the code word for a world of repressed passion between Edna and Robert that Mademoiselle Reisz controls. Later the pianist plays a Chopin im-promptu for Edna that Robert has admired; this time the music is "strange and fantastic – turbulent, plaintive and soft with entreaty" (Chap. 21). These references to "Chopin" in the text are on one level allusions to an intimate, romantic, and poignant musical *oeuvre* that reinforces the novel's sensual atmosphere. But on an-other level, they function as what Nancy K. Miller has called the "internal female signature" in women's writing, here a literary punning signature that alludes to Kate Chopin's ambitions as an artist and to the emotions she wished her book to arouse in its readers.[33]

Chopin's career represented one important aesthetic model for his literary namesake. As a girl, Kate Chopin had been a talented musician, and her first published story, "Wiser Than a God," was about a woman concert pianist who refused to marry. Moreover, Chopin's music both stylistically and thematically influences the language and form of *The Awakening*. The structure of the im-promptu, in which there is an opening presentation of a theme, a contrasting middle section, and a modified return to the melodic and rhythmic materials of the opening section, parallels the nar-rative form of *The Awakening*. The composer's techniques of unify-ing his work through the repetition of musical phrases, his experi-ments with harmony and dissonance, his use of folk motifs, his effects of frustration and delayed resolution can also be compared to Kate Chopin's repetition of sentences, her juxtaposition of real-ism and impressionism, her incorporation of local color elements, and her rejection of conventional closure. Like that of the com-poser's impromptu, Chopin's style seems spontaneous and im-provised, but it is in fact carefully designed and executed.[34]

Madame Ratignolle and Mademoiselle Reisz not only represent important alternative roles and influences for Edna in the world of the novel, but as the proto-heroines of sentimental and local color fiction, they also suggest different plots and conclusions. Adele's story suggests that Edna will give up her rebellion, return to her marriage, have another baby, and by degrees learn to appreciate, love, and even desire her husband. Such was the plot of many late-nineteenth-century sentimental novels about erring young women married to older men, such as Susan Warner's *Diana* (1880) and Louisa May Alcott's *Moods* (1882). Mademoiselle Reisz's story suggests that Edna will lose her beauty, her youth, her husband, and children – everything, in short, but her art and her pride – and become a kind of New Orleans nun.

Chopin wished to reject both of these endings and to escape from the literary traditions they represented; but her own literary solitude, her resistance to allying herself with a specific ideological or aesthetic position, made it impossible for her to work out something different and new. Edna remains very much entangled in her own emotions and moods, rather than moving beyond them to real self-understanding and to an awareness of her relationship to her society. She alternates between two moods of "intoxication" and "languor," expansive states of activity, optimism, and power and passive states of contemplation, despondency, and sexual thralldom. Edna feels intoxicated when she is assertive and in control. She first experiences such exultant feelings when she confides her history to Adele Ratignolle and again when she learns how to swim: "intoxicated with her newly conquered power," she swims out too far. She is excited when she gambles successfully for high stakes at the race track, and finally she feels "an intoxication of expectancy" about awakening Robert with a seductive kiss and playing the dominant role with him. But these emotional peaks are countered by equally intense moods of depression, reverie, or stupor. At the worst, these are states of "indescribable oppression," "vague anguish," or "hopeless ennui." At best, they are moments of passive sensuality in which Edna feels drugged; Arobin's lips and hands, for example, act "like a narcotic upon her" (Chap. 25).

Edna welcomes both kinds of feelings because they are intense, and thus preserve her from the tedium of ordinary existence. They are in fact adolescent emotions, suitable to a heroine who is belatedly awakening; but Edna does not go beyond them to an adulthood that offers new experiences or responsibilities. In her relationships with men, she both longs for complete and romantic fusion with a fantasy lover and is unprepared to share her life with another person.

Chopin's account of the Pontellier marriage, for example, shows Edna's tacit collusion in a sexual bargain that allows her to keep to herself. Although she thinks of her marriage to a paternalistic man twelve years her senior as "purely an accident," the text makes it clear that Edna has married Leonce primarily to secure a fatherly protector who will not make too many domestic, emotional, or sexual demands on her. She is "fond of her husband," with "no trace of passion or excessive or fictitious warmth" (Chap. 7). They do not have an interest in each other's activities or thoughts, and have agreed to a complete separation of their social spheres; Leonce is fully absorbed by the business, social, and sexual activities of the male sphere, the city, Carondelet Street, Klein's Hotel at Grand Isle, where he gambles, and especially the New Orleans world of the clubs and the red-light district. Even Adele Ratignolle warns Edna of the risks of Mr. Pontellier's club life and of the "diversion" he finds there. "It's a pity Mr. Pontellier doesn't stay home more in the evenings," she tells Edna. "I think you would be more – well, if you don't mind my saying it – more united, if he did." "Oh! dear no!" Edna responds, "with a blank look in her eyes. 'What should I do if he stayed home? We wouldn't have anything to say to each other'" (Chap. 23). Edna gets this blank look in her eyes – eyes that are originally described as "quick and bright" – whenever she is confronted with something she does not want to see. When she joins the Ratignolles at home together, Edna does not envy them, although, as the author remarks, "if ever the fusion of two human beings into one has been accomplished on this sphere it was surely in their union" (Chap. 18). Instead, she is moved by pity for Adele's "colorless existence which never uplifted its possessor beyond the region of blind contentment" (Chap. 18).

Nonetheless, Edna does not easily relinquish her fantasy of rhapsodic oneness with a perfect lover. She imagines that such a union will bring permanent ecstasy; it will lead, not simply to "domestic harmony" like that of the Ratignolles, but to "life's delirium" (Chap. 18). In her story of the woman who paddles away with her lover in a pirogue and is never heard of again, Edna elaborates on her vision as she describes the lovers, "close together, rapt in oblivious forgetfulness, drifting into the unknown" (Chap. 23). Although her affair with Arobin shocks her into an awareness of her own sexual passions, it leaves her illusions about love intact. Desire, she understands, can exist independently of love. But love retains its magical aura; indeed, her sexual awakening with Arobin generates an even "fiercer, more overpowering love" for Robert (Chap. 28). And when Robert comes back, Edna has persuaded herself that the force of their love will overwhelm all obstacles: "We shall be everything to each other. Nothing else in the world is of any consequence" (Chap. 36). Her intention seems to be that they will go off together into the unknown, like the lovers in her story. But Robert cannot accept such a role, and when he leaves her, Edna finally realizes "that the day would come when he, too, and the thought of him, would melt out of her existence, leaving her alone" (Chap. 39).

The other side of Edna's terror of solitude, however, is the bondage of class as well as gender that keeps her in a prison of the self. She goes blank too whenever she might be expected to notice the double standard of ladylike privilege and oppression of women in southern society. Floating along in her "mazes of inward contemplation," Edna barely notices the silent quadroon nurse who takes care of her children, the little black girl who works the treadles of Madame Lebrun's sewing machine, the laundress who keeps her in frilly white, or the maid who picks up her broken glass. She never makes connections between her lot and theirs.

The scene in which Edna witnesses Adele in childbirth (Chap. 37) is the first time in the novel that she identifies with another woman's pain, and draws some halting conclusions about the female and the human condition, rather than simply about her own ennui. Edna's births have taken place in unconsciousness; when she goes to Adele's childbed, "her own like experiences seemed far away, unreal, and only half remembered. She recalled faintly an ecstasy of pain, the heavy odor of chloroform, a stupor which had deadened sensation" (Chap. 37) The stupor that deadens sensation is an apt metaphor for the real and imaginary narcotics supplied by fantasy, money, and patriarchy, which have protected Edna from pain for most of her life, but which have also kept her from becoming an adult.

But in thinking of nature's trap for women, Edna never moves from her own questioning to the larger social statement that is feminism. Her ineffectuality is partly a product of her time; as a heroine in transition between the homosocial and the heterosexual worlds, Edna has lost some of the sense of connectedness to other women that might help her plan her future. Though she has sojourned in the "female colony" of Grand Isle, it is far from being a feminist utopia, a real community of women, in terms of sisterhood. The novel suggests, in fact, something of the historical loss for women of transferring the sense of self to relationships with men.

Edna's solitude is one of the reasons that her emancipation does not take her very far. Despite her efforts to escape the rituals of femininity, Edna seems fated to reenact them, even though, as Chopin recounts these scenes, she satirizes and revises their conventions. Ironically, considering her determination to discard the trappings of her role as a society matron – her wedding ring, her "reception day," her "charming home" – the high point of Edna's awakening is the dinner party she gives for her twenty-ninth birthday. Edna's birthday party begins like a kind of drawing-room comedy. We are told the guest list, the seating plan, the menu, and the table setting; some of the guests are boring, and some do not like each other; Madame Ratignolle does not show up at the last minute, and Mademoiselle Reisz makes disagreeable remarks in French.

Yet as it proceeds to its bacchanalian climax, the dinner party also has a symbolic intensity and resonance that makes it, as Sandra Gilbert argues, Edna's "most authentic act of self-definition."[35] Not only is the twenty-ninth birthday a feminine threshold, the passage from youth to middle age, but Edna is literally on the threshold of a new life in her little house. The dinner, as Arobin remarks, is a *coup d'état*, an overthrow of her marriage, all the more an act of aggression because Leonce will pay the bills. Moreover, she has created an atmosphere of splendor and luxury that seems to exceed the requirements of the occasion. The table is set with gold satin, Sevres china, crystal, silver, and gold; there is "champagne to swim in" (Chap. 29), and Edna is magnificently dressed in a satin and lace gown, with a cluster of diamonds (a gift from Leonce) in her hair. Presiding at the head of the table, she seems powerful and autonomous: "There was something in her attitude which suggested the regal woman, the one who rules, who looks on, who stands alone" (Chap. 30). Edna's moment of mastery thus takes place in the context of a familiar ceremony of women's culture. Indeed, dinner parties are virtual set pieces of feminist aesthetics, suggesting that the hostess is a kind of artist in her own sphere, someone whose creativity is channeled into the production of social and domestic harmony. Like Virginia Woolf's Mrs. Ramsay in *To the Lighthouse*, Edna exhausts herself in creating a sense of fellowship at her table, although in the midst of her guests she still experiences an "acute longing" for "the unattainable" (Chap. 30).

But there is a gap between the intensity of Edna's desire, a desire that by now has gone beyond sexual fulfillment to take in a much vaster range of metaphysical longings, and the means that she has to express herself. Edna may look like a queen, but she is still a housewife. The political and aesthetic weapons she has in her *coup d'état* are only forks and knives, glasses and dresses.

Can Edna, and Kate Chopin, then, escape from confining traditions only in death? Some critics have seen Edna's much-debated suicide as a heroic embrace of independence and a symbolic resurrection into myth, a feminist counterpart of Melville's Bulkington: "Take heart, take heart, O Edna, up from the spray of thy ocean-perishing, up, straight up, leaps thy apotheosis!" But the ending too seems to return Edna to the nineteenth-century female literary tradition, even though Chopin redefines it for her own purpose. Readers of the 1890s were well accustomed to drowning as the fictional punishment for female transgression against morality, and most contemporary critics of *The Awakening* thus automatically interpreted Edna's suicide as the wages of sin.

Drowning itself brings to mind metaphorical analogies between femininity and liquidity. As the female body is prone to wetness, blood, milk, tears, and amniotic fluid, so in drowning the woman is immersed in the feminine organic element. Drowning thus becomes the traditionally feminine literary death.[36] And Edna's last

52

thoughts further recycle significant images of the feminine from her past. As exhaustion overpowers her, "Edna heard her father's voice and her sister Margaret's. She heard the barking of an old dog that was chained to the sycamore tree. The spurs of the cavalry officer clanged as he walked across the porch. There was the hum of bees, and the musky odor of pinks filled the air" (Chap. 39). Edna's memories are those of awakening from the freedom of childhood to the limitations conferred by female sexuality.

The image of the bees and the flowers not only recalls early descriptions of Edna's sexuality as a "sensitive blossom," but also places *The Awakening* firmly within the traditions of American women's writing, where it is a standard trope for the unequal sexual relations between women and men. Margaret Fuller, for example, writes in her journal: "Woman is the flower, man the bee. She sighs out of melodious fragrance, and invites the winged laborer. He drains her cup, and carries off the honey. She dies on the stalk; he returns to the hive, well fed, and praised as an active member of the community."[37] In post–Civil War fiction, the image is a reminder of an elemental power that women's culture must confront. *The Awakening* seems particularly to echo the last lines of Mary Wilkins Freeman's "A New England Nun," in which the heroine, having broken her long-standing engagement, is free to continue her solitary life, and closes her door on "the sounds of the busy harvest of men and birds and bees; there were halloos, metallic clatterings, sweet calls, long hummings."[38] These are the images of a nature that, Edna has learned, decoys women into slavery; yet even in drowning, she cannot escape from their seductiveness, for to ignore their claim is also to cut oneself off from culture, from the "humming" life of creation and achievement.

We can re-create the literary tradition in which Kate Chopin wrote *The Awakening*, but of course, we can never know how the tradition might have changed if her novel had not had to wait half a century to find its audience. Few of Chopin's literary contemporaries came into contact with the book. Chopin's biographer, Per Seyersted, notes that her work "was apparently unknown to Dreiser, even though he began writing *Sister Carrie* just when *The Awakening* was being loudly condemned. Also Ellen Glasgow, who was at this time beginning to describe unsatisfactory marriages, seems to have been unaware of the author's existence. Indeed, we can safely say that though she was so much of an innovator in American literature, she was virtually unknown by those who were now to shape it and that she had no influence on them."[39] Ironically, even Willa Cather, the one woman writer of the *fin-de-siècle* who reviewed *The Awakening*, not only failed to recognize its importance but also dismissed its theme as "trite."[40] It would be decades before another American woman novelist combined Kate Chopin's artistic maturity with her sophisticated outlook on sexuality, and overcame both the sentimental codes of feminine "artlessness" and the sexual codes of feminine "passionlessness."

In terms of Chopin's own literary development, there were signs that *The Awakening* would have been a pivotal work. While it was in press, she wrote one of her finest and most daring short stories, "The Storm," which surpasses even *The Awakening* in terms of its expressive freedom. Chopin was also being drawn back to a rethinking of women's culture. Her last poem, written in 1900, was addressed to Kitty Garesché and spoke of the permanence of emotional bonds between women:

To the Friend of My Youth

It is not all of life
To cling together while the years glide past.
It is not all of love
To walk with clasped hands from the first to last.
That mystic garland which the spring did twine
Of scented lilac and the new-blown rose,
Faster than chains will hold my soul to thine
Thro' joy, and grief, thro' life – unto its close.[41]

We have only these tantalizing fragments to hint at the directions Chopin's work might have taken if *The Awakening* had been a critical success or even a *succès de scandale,* and if her career had not been cut off by her early death. The fate of *The Awakening* shows only too well how a literary tradition may be enabling, even essential, as well as confining. Struggling to escape from tradition, Kate Chopin courageously risked social and literary ostracism. It is up to contemporary readers to restore her solitary book to its place in our literary heritage.

NOTES

1. Guy de Maupassant, "Solitude," trans. Kate Chopin, *St. Louis Life* 12 (December 28, 1895), 30; quoted in Margaret Culley, "Edna Pontellier: 'A Solitary Soul,'" in *The Awakening*, Norton Critical Edition (New York: Norton, 1976), p. 224.
2. See the contemporary reviews in the Norton Critical Edition, pp. 145–55.
3. "Confidences," in *The Complete Works of Kate Chopin*, ed. Per Seyersted (Baton Rouge: Louisiana State University Press, 1969), Vol. II, p. 701.
4. Carroll Smith-Rosenberg, *Disorderly Conduct: Visions of Gender in Victorian America* (New York: Knopf, 1985), p. 28.
5. Nancy R. Cott, "Passionlessness: An Interpretation of Victorian Sexual Ideology, 1790–1850," *Signs* 4 (1978):233.
6. Catherine Maria Sedgwick, manuscript diary, quoted in Cott, "Passionlessness," 233.
7. Smith-Rosenberg, *Disorderly Conduct*, p. 69.
8. See Mary P. Ryan, *The Empire of the Mother: American Writing about Domesticity* (New York: Haworth Press, 1982).
9. Harriet Beecher Stowe, *My Wife and I*, quoted in Mary Kelley, *Private Woman, Public Stage: Literary Domesticity in Nineteenth-Century America* (New York: Oxford University Press, 1984), p. 327.
10. Ibid., p. 249.
11. Mary P. Ryan, *Womanhood in America from Colonial Times to the Present* (New York: Franklin Watts, 1983), p. 144.
12. Nina Baym, *Women's Fiction: A Guide to Novels by and about Women in America 1820–1870* (Ithaca, N.Y.: Cornell University Press, 1978), p. 32.
13. Ibid., p. 32.
14. Elizabeth Stuart Phelps, "Art for Truth's Sake," in her autobiography, *Chapters from a Life* (Boston: Houghton Mifflin, 1897).
15. Sarah Orne Jewett, *Letters*, ed. Annie Adams Field (Boston: Houghton Mifflin, 1911), p. 47; quoted in Josephine Donovan, *Sarah Orne Jewett* (New York: Frederick Ungar, 1980), p. 124.
16. Susan B. Anthony, "Homes of Single Women," 1877, quoted in Carol Farley Kessler, "Introduction" to Elizabeth Stuart Phelps, *The*

Story of Avis (repr. New Brunswick, N.J.: Rutgers University Press, 1985), xxii.

17. Phelps, *The Story of Avis,* pp. 126, 246.
18. Elizabeth Cady Stanton, diary for 1883, quoted in Cott, "Passionlessness," 236 n. 60.
19. Linda Dowling, "The Decadent and the New Woman in the 1890s," *Nineteenth-Century Fiction* 33 (1979):441.
20. Frances Porcher, "Kate Chopin's Novel," *The Mirror* (May 4, 1899) and "Books of the Day," *Chicago Times-Herald* (June 1, 1899), in Norton Critical Edition, pp. 145, 149.
21. Martha Vicinus, "Introduction" to George Egerton, *Keynotes and Discords* (repr. London: Virago Books, 1983), xvi.
22. George Egerton, "A Keynote to *Keynotes,*" in *Ten Contemporaries,* ed. John Gawsworth (London: Ernest Benn, 1932), p. 60.
23. Per Seyersted, *Kate Chopin: A Critical Biography* (New York: Octagon Books, 1980), p. 18.
24. Sandra Gilbert, "Introduction" to *The Awakening and Selected Stories* (Harmondsworth: Penguin, 1984), p. 16.
25. "Confidences," in Chopin, *Complete Works* Vol. II, pp. 700–1.
26. "Crumbling Idols," in Chopin, *Complete Works,* Vol. II, p. 693.
27. Seyersted, *Kate Chopin,* p. 83.
28. Ibid., p. 58.
29. Ibid., p. 209, n. 55.
30. "Confidences," in Chopin, *Complete Works,* Vol. II, p. 702.
31. Henry James, November 26, 1892, quoted in Larzer Ziff, *The American 1890s* (New York: Viking, 1966), p. 275.
32. Gilbert, "Introduction," p. 25.
33. Thanks to Nancy K. Miller of Barnard College for this phrase from her current work on the development of women's writing in France. I am also indebted to the insights of Cheryl Torsney of the University of West Virginia, and to the comments of the other participants of my NEH Seminar on "Women's Writing and Women's Culture," Summer 1984.
34. Thanks to Lynne Rogers, Music Department, Princeton University, for information about Frédéric Chopin.
35. Gilbert, "Introduction," p. 30.
36. See Gaston Bachelard, *L'eau et les rêves* (Paris, 1942), pp. 109–25.
37. Margaret Fuller, "Life Without and Life Within," quoted in Bell G. Chevigny, *The Woman and the Myth* (Old Westbury, N.Y.: Feminist Press, 1976), p. 349. See also Wendy Martin, *An American Triptych:*

Anne Bradstreet, Emily Dickinson, Adrienne Rich (Chapel Hill: University of North Carolina Press, 1984), pp. 154–9.

38. "A New England Nun," in Mary Wilkins Freeman, *The Revolt of Mother*, ed. Michele Clark (New York: Feminist Press, 1974), p. 97.

39. Seyersted, *Kate Chopin*, p. 196.

40. "Sibert" [Willa Cather], "Books and Magazines," *Pittsburgh Leader* (July 8, 1899), in Norton Critical Edition, p. 153.

41. Chopin, *Complete Works*, Vol. II, p. 735.

3

Revolt Against Nature: The Problematic Modernism of *The Awakening*

MICHAEL T. GILMORE

1

WHEN Adele Ratignolle gives birth in Chapter 37 of *The Awakening,* Kate Chopin writes that her heroine, Edna Pontellier, witnesses the suffering of her friend "with an inward agony, with a flaming, outspoken revolt against the ways of Nature." Of all the verities against which Edna sets herself in shattering her conventional marriage – the religion of domesticity, the family, property, the social order itself – none enjoyed greater prestige in late-nineteenth-century American culture than "Nature," a word Chopin capitalizes as though she were referring to Providence or the Supreme Being. Indeed, one might justifiably regard the natural as the privileged category undergirding almost all of those institutions venerated by Edna's and Chopin's contemporaries. Within the novel, Dr. Mandelet underscores nature's centrality as the impediment to Edna's self-realization when he and Edna leave the Ratignolle home together after Adele's ordeal. "Youth is given up to illusions," sighs the doctor. "It seems to be a provision of Nature; a decoy to secure mothers for the race. And Nature takes no account of moral consequences, of arbitrary conditions which we create, and which we feel obliged to maintain at any cost" (Chap. 38).

Edna's "revolt" takes place within the larger context of a crisis in her culture's perception of nature, a crisis that deeply troubled Americans, though it was not confined to this country. There developed a widespread feeling around the turn of the century that Western civilization had lost touch with nature and was consequently entering or, in the more pessimistic assessments, already well advanced toward a state of decay. The New Woman, of which Edna is a version, was considered a symptom of the crisis. By

59

demanding changes in marriage and practices of child rearing, feminists like Charlotte Perkins Gilman gave notice of their determination to alter what many took to be the natural order of things. But the questioning of women's traditional role was not more worrisome to Americans than the threats to the polity and the economy represented by the closing of the frontier and the rise of huge corporations. Like the criticism of the family, these events seemed to stem from an attenuation of the nation's historic source of strength, its special tie to the physical environment. The conservation movement, the cult of outdoor life associated with Teddy Roosevelt, and the campaign to regulate the trusts were all part of the *fin-de-siècle* effort to reinvigorate the natural values Edna wishes to overthrow.[1]

The question of fidelity or infidelity to nature also became a matter of paramount concern in the arts at this time. In the United States, which lagged behind Europe artistically, realists like William Dean Howells and Mark Twain dominated the cultural scene and saw their task as one of encouraging "life-likeness" in literature while reproving romantic inaccuracies.[2] In Europe, which was experiencing the first stirrings of modernism, a shift away from the imitation of natural appearance had already occurred – for example, in the paintings of the Impressionists, who emphasized the artist's response to what he saw as much as the object itself. A writer steeped in European, and particularly French, culture, Chopin in her fiction moves away from a strict adherence to "the outside of men and things."[3] She situates her novel and its heroine in critical and often subversive relation to the mimetic ideal. In *The Awakening*, a book dense with references to painting, photography, and music, as well as literature, Chopin draws a parallel between realistic or representational aesthetics and the constraining model of marriage admired by late Victorian society.

Chopin's feminist narrative marks a turn toward the anti-naturalist, self-referential agenda of modernism as a liberating mode of behavior in life and art. Yet neither Edna nor Chopin achieves such liberation, and not simply because of the heroine's suicide. Both women remain trapped in habits of thought they oppose, conceptual systems that prove so pertinacious that they saturate the very act of opposition. Edna, who struggles to free

60

herself from her society's ideal of female identity, never relinquishes a limiting Victorian notion of what constitutes a "real" self. And Chopin, in her quest for escape from representation, reverts to nature as a pattern to be imitated. She unwittingly makes clear that Edna's sense of selfhood as an awakened being paradoxically rests on the same ideology of likeness that she and the heroine reject as antithetical to genuine individuality.

2

No book published in America in 1899 with a title like *The Awakening* could have failed to arouse specific expectations in the reading public. The expectations would almost certainly have been religious: Revivals of faith or "great awakenings" have been common throughout American history, and the title would immediately have suggested the dawning of spiritual consciousness. As James D. Hart points out in his study of American best-sellers, books with precisely this kind of religious theme were extremely popular in the nineties.[4] But Chopin's novel is, of course, the narrative of an antireligious awakening, the emotional and sexual enlightenment of a married woman who, attaining "more wisdom than the Holy Ghost is usually pleased to vouchsafe to any woman" (Chap. 6), takes a lover and kills herself rather than resume her respectable existence.

Religion is just one of the certainties Edna unsettles in the course of her development. Her instinctive antipathy to Christianity – she is constantly fleeing church services – derives in part from her awareness of its alliance with the traditional family structure. Religion lends its authority to what Charlotte Perkins Gilman, writing a year before Edna's self-discovery, described as "the doctrine of maternal sacrifice," the "devout belief" that one-half of humanity ought to surrender "all other human interests and activities to concentrate its time, strength, and devotion upon the functions of maternity."[5] The "mother-women" Edna knows at Grand Isle renounce their separate identities with quasi-religious fervor. "They were women who idolized their children, worshiped their husbands, and esteemed it a holy privilege to efface themselves as individuals and grow wings as ministering angels" (Chap. 4).

Madame Ratignolle, who has the appearance and manner of "a faultless Madonna" (Chap. 5), is the embodiment of self-abnegating motherhood. Edna shocks her friend when she declares that "she would never sacrifice herself for her children, or for any one" (Chap. 16). She comes to see her husband and two boys not as the reason for her existence but rather as antagonists who seek to thwart her growth and "drag her into the soul's slavery for the rest of her days" (Chap. 39).

Edna's revolt against the family also constitutes a threat to property. This is so because women have been customarily thought of as belonging to men. Hence Leonce Pontellier looks at his sun-burned wife "as one looks at a valuable piece of personal property which has suffered some damage" (Chap. 1), and he treasures her much as he does his other possessions, "chiefly because they were his" (Chap. 17). The denial to women of autonomous or initiating selfhood, and their reduction to the status of persons owned by others, is so prevalent a condition in Creole society that it is un-critically endorsed by Robert Lebrun even though he would like to marry Edna. He is perplexed and alarmed when she dismisses the notion of her husband setting her free: "I am no longer one of Mr. Pontellier's possessions to dispose of or not. I give myself where I choose. If he were to say, 'Here, Robert, take her and be happy; she is yours,' I should laugh at you both" (Chap. 36).

Edna resolves to commit suicide because she can find no room for her newly awakened self in the present social system. To return to her former life would be to permit her husband and children "to possess her, body and soul" (Chap. 39), and she is determined never again to subordinate her individuality to others. Alcée Arobin expresses a fundamental truth of the novel when he char-acterizes the dinner party Edna gives to celebrate moving into her own house as a *"coup d'état"* (Chap. 39). Her quest for self-fulfill-ment, though it ends in death, is an insurrectionary act because it calls a civilization into question; it has to end in death because there is no way for the world she inhabits to accommodate the change in her. In this sense *The Awakening* belongs to the classic tradition of American novels in which the hero or heroine – Hester Prynne, Ishmael, Huck Finn – challenges less a particular institution than the entire organization of society. Unlike those figures, who fly to the margins of the community, Edna is not an outcast; unlike them again, her disaffection proves so total that she takes her life instead of allowing herself to be reintegrated into the existing order. Nothing less than a transformation of social reality would enable the "new-born creature" (Chap. 39) Edna has become to go on living.

Chopin thoroughly immerses Edna's story in the upper-middle-class world of the late nineteenth century. The exquisite, detailed rendering of life among the affluent is what gives the book its distinctive texture, and Edna's growing sense of entrapment does not prevent her from taking pleasure in many aspects of leisure-class existence. Events unfold against a background of elegant homes and secluded resorts. Chopin's writing conveys the sensual richness of these settings, as in her description of the beach at Grand Isle, reached by sandy paths among acres of yellow camomile and glistening clumps of orange and lemon trees; or her account of the table setting for Edna's dinner party, with its profusion of red and yellow roses, "cover of pale yellow satin under strips of lace-work," and "wax candles in massive brass candelabra, burning softly under yellow silk shades" (Chap. 30). Since a good part of the action occurs during the long summer vacation on the Gulf, people are shown amusing themselves at activities like swimming, strolling on the beach, attending musical *soirees,* and taking excursions to exotic islands. Servants, seemingly always colored, are everywhere, from the quadroon who looks after the Pontellier boys on Grand Isle, to the cook who spoils Leonce's soup in New Orleans, to the black woman, Old Celestine, who accompanies Edna to the pigeon house and prepares her meals for her.

The Awakening gives unusual emphasis to the consumption of food, as if to highlight the importance in middle-class life of appetite and its gratification. Many crucial scenes involve eating: Edna and her husband clash over her supervision of the cook; Dr. Mandelet senses Edna's passionate yearnings while he dines at the Pontelliers; the *coup d'état* is a sumptuous feast for ten; and Robert and Edna meet unexpectedly at an out-of-the-way restaurant in the suburbs after his return from Mexico. Although Edna herself never cooks, leaving household chores to the servants, she differs from most Victorian heroines of her social class in that she enjoys food and has no inhibitions about making known her desire for it.[6] Chopin accentuates the physicality of her eating, as when she awakens famished from her nap at the Chenière Caminada: "Edna bit a piece from the brown loaf, tearing it with her strong, white teeth. She poured some of the wine into the glass and drank it down" (Chap. 13). Edna's appetite is unrepressed to the end of her life; she asks Victor Lebrun to have fresh fish prepared for dinner moments before she drowns herself in the Gulf.

The lush, sensuous ambiance of Chopin's novel is notably similar to that of the world portrayed in Impressionist paintings of two or three decades earlier. The resemblance extends both to subject matter and to technique. Meyer Schapiro has commented on "how many pictures we have in early Impressionism of informal and spontaneous sociability, of breakfasts, picnics, promenades, boating trips, holidays and vacation travel."[7] Canvases like Manet's *Déjeuner sur l'herbe* (1863) and Seurat's *A Sunday Afternoon on the Island of La Grande Jatte* (1884–6) strongly evoke Chopin's work. Chopin also suggests the Impressionists in her interest in creating atmosphere through sensory imagery, particularly color and light. From the first sentence, which refers to "a green and yellow parrot," she flecks her pages with vivid dabs of paint. Like Edna, whose love of sunbathing so exasperates her husband, the book's prose seems "to be one with the sunlight, the color, the odors, the luxuriant warmth of some perfect Southern day" (Chap. 19).

More telling than these surface affinities is the deeper kinship between Edna's evolving state of mind and the objectives of Impressionist art. Rather than aspiring to an unmediated vision of reality, Impressionism is concerned with a given scene's effect on the individual consciousness; by giving priority to the sensations of the artist, it actively disfigures or decomposes the external world. Shapes tend to lose their solid form as they change and blur in accordance with the shifting position or feelings of the observer. The spontaneous is preferred to the static, the momentary accorded a higher value than the permanent. Schapiro asserts that Impressionism's "unconventionalized, unregulated vision" implies "a criticism of symbolic social and domestic formalities, or at least a norm opposed to these."[8] So understood, Impressionist painting can be viewed as the aesthetic analogue to Edna's jettisoning of religion, family, and community as a result of her awakening. Outer reality in the novel undergoes a radical destabilization as she yields to passing sensations and becomes increasingly a prey to moods. Chopin writes that "she was seeing with different eyes and making the acquaintance of new conditions in herself that colored and changed her environment" (Chap. 14). Unwilling to suppress her emerging self, she begins "to do as she liked and to feel as she liked" (Chap. 19). In responding to the demands of her inner nature, Edna discovers the sensibility of an Impressionist painter and dissolves the external structures of her world.

Where Edna and the Impressionists most agree, then, is in their common turning inward, their transfer of allegiance from the outer world to the personality and freedom of the individual. For the Impressionists, this transfer involved a partial emancipation from the authority of natural forms. As Cézanne put it, "I have not tried to reproduce Nature. . . . Art should not imitate nature, but should express the sensations aroused by nature."[9] But though Impressionism is part of the general trend in modern art toward abstraction and the primacy of inner feelings, it remains bound to recognizable objects such as haystacks and water lilies; its break with representation is incomplete. Edna and Chopin are ultimately unable to transcend the Impressionist compromise, yet they nonetheless strive to go beyond it and to achieve something approximating the modernist escape from everyday reality. Both women wish to find a way out of the "fettering tradition of nature,"[10] and both aspire to speak, like the brightly colored parrot introduced on the novel's first page, "a language which nobody understood" (Chap. 1).

3

The parrot, a key symbol, has a number of meanings, some of them contradictory. The bird's mastery of an incomprehensible language serves as a model for Chopin and her heroine, but along with the mockingbird also mentioned on the first page, the parrot is a "caged imitator"[11] and thus the very thing Edna determines not to be when she spurns the role of selfless mother-woman, "fluttering about with extended, protecting wings" (Chap. 4). As a novelist, Chopin is equally intent upon shunning mimicry; her ambition is to write a genuinely original book, not to repeat what others have written before her. She observes of Adele Ratignolle, "There are no words to describe her save the old ones that have served so often to picture the by-gone heroine of romance and the fair lady of our dreams." Adele has "spun-gold hair," "blue eyes . . . like nothing but sapphires," and lips "so red one could only think of cherries" (Chap. 4). This overused, trite language denies individuality as surely as the typical Creole marriage, and Chopin wants no part of it in describing Edna, the present-day heroine of a new kind of story.

The desire for an authentic language is thematized in *The Awakening* through Edna's search for self-expression, a search that brings her into conflict with the linguistic usages of Creole society. The Creoles are outwardly uninhibited in their speech, often causing Edna to redden with their frank conversation about intimate matters like childbirth. They openly read and discuss a daring book that she hastily removes from sight when anyone comes near. "Their freedom of expression," says Chopin, "was at first incomprehensible to her" (Chap. 4). But this apparent candor is misleading: Language among the Creoles may be unencumbered by prudery, but it lacks sincerity as well. Robert speaks "words of love to Madame Ratignolle, without any thought of being taken seriously" (Chap. 5), and Arobin, whose verbal effrontery arouses Edna, habitually says things to women that he doesn't mean.

Edna differs from the Creoles in that she respects words and tries to use them accurately, so as to express her individuality. Accustomed "to harbor thoughts and emotions which never voiced themselves" (Chap. 16), she begins to shed her verbal inhibition and to utter sentiments unintelligible to her companions. When she tells Adele that she wouldn't sacrifice herself for her children, Chopin writes that "the two women did not appear to understand each other or to be talking the same language" (Chap. 16). Adele's bafflement is later matched by Robert's; Edna is now the one whose "freedom of expression" is incomprehensible, and she thoroughly exposes the falsity of the Creole claim to liberated speech. After Robert returns from Mexico, she brings a flush to his face – it was she who used to do the blushing – by confronting him about his failure to write. And when she asks him what he has been feeling during his absence, and he puts her off with a generality, she repeats his words verbatim, satirizing Creole verbal practices by both parroting and mocking him for his evasion (Chap. 23).

Edna's drive to experience and articulate her inner life dooms her to incomprehension because the very idea of a wife having a separate and unique identity is alien to Creole culture. The ideal Creole couple like the Ratignolles are in such perfect harmony with each other that jealousy or misunderstanding is impossible. "The right hand jealous of the left! The heart jealous of the soul!" (Chap. 5). By means of these comparisons, Chopin indicates how absurd it would be for a Creole husband to doubt his wife's loyalty; emotionally the two are almost indistinguishable, much as one hand is the duplicate of the other. As a later passage has it, "If ever the fusion of two human beings into one has been accomplished on this sphere it was surely in their union." This unity carries over into language, where every word the spouses exchange is totally transparent: "The Ratignolles understood each other perfectly." In fact, the model Creole wife is a kind of verbal plagiarist, striving to be as alike in speech as she is in her emotions. Adele literally parrots her husband at the dinner table, drinking in everything he says, "laying down her fork the better to listen, chiming in, taking the words out of his mouth" (Chap. 18). Edna, who feels stifled by the expectation of marital likeness, turns her own marriage into a linguistic battlefield. She bristles at her husband's commands, warning him, "Don't speak to me like that again; I shall not answer you" (Chap. 11); and when Adele proposes that the Pontelliers would be more "united" if they spent more time together, she objects, "We wouldn't have anything to say to each other" (Chap. 23).

The perfection of union between the Ratignolles, with the wife a mirror image of the husband, implies a representational aesthetic. Chopin makes Adele the advocate of such an aesthetic within the novel. Edna, who has a natural talent for painting, attempts to sketch her friend at Grand Isle, and the finished portrait is said to bear "no resemblance to Madame Ratignolle," who "was greatly disappointed to find that it did not look like her" (Chap. 5). Just as she espouses affinity between husband and wife, so Adele craves likeness in works of art; she believes there should be complete agreement between image and object, the representation and the thing represented. Fidelity, to one's spouse and to nature, is the governing principle of her thought. Chopin underlies this point in Chapter 18: Within the space of three paragraphs she describes the fusion of the Ratignolle marriage and then has Adele exclaim over the realism of Edna's later sketches — a realism so exact, in Adele's view, that the sign seems at one with the referent. "Surely, this Bavarian peasant is worthy of framing; and this basket of apples! never have I seen anything more lifelike. One might almost be tempted to reach out a hand and take one" (Chap. 18).[12] Adele's attitude again evokes the parrot in its imitative mode — not the parrot as verbal echo now but as a figure for the accurate representation of reality. She admires the wife who replicates the husband and artwork that faithfully reproduces physical appearance.

Chopin's insight that likeness is the common ground of Western marriage and mimetic art suggests that her own unorthodoxy as a writer is closely allied to Edna's discontent. Although *The Awakening* is a realist novel in many respects, it mounts a series of challenges to the ideology of representation, and it violates contemporary aesthetic standards both in what it dares to say and how it tells its story. Like Edna's, Chopin's frankness offended moral sensibilities, and the consequences were almost as disastrous for her as for her heroine. Edna's career of sexual and linguistic trespasses ends in suicide; for Chopin, the result of publishing *The Awakening* was her demise as a professional author. Early reviewers showed near unanimity in judging the story morbid and unhealthy, dealing with matters better left unsaid; several admitted a wish that the novel had never been written.[13] Chopin was crushed by the hostile critical reaction, which destroyed her career and effectively silenced her. Her book was banned from the public libraries of St. Louis, her native city, and a collection of tales, originally accepted for publication along with *The Awakening*, was returned without explanation by the publishers. Only two more of Chopin's stories reached print before her death in 1904, and she suffered fifty years of critical neglect for having ventured to speak "a language which nobody understood."[14]

There were many reasons why Chopin's openness about female sexuality proved unacceptable to her contemporaries. Her willingness to treat adultery without condemning it seemed to some reviewers to betray a covert sympathy for Edna's conduct. Another objection, voiced by Willa Cather, reflected a consensus among American realists. Cather's strictures centered on the exaggerated attention paid to the passion of love. People like Edna Pontellier, she complained, expect love "to fill and gratify every need of life, whereas nature only intended that it should meet one of many demands."[15] Edna's behavior, in other words, was romantic and unnatural; indeed, William Dean Howells, the leading American proponent of realism, would have found the entire novel an inaccurate record of life. Although Howells did not review *The Awakening*, his manifesto of 1891, *Criticism and Fiction*, set forth in advance his disapproval of what it represented. Addressing the supposed limitation that "an American novelist may not write a story on the lines of Anna Karenina or Madame Bovary," Howells disputed the usual contention that "the Young Girl," the principal audience for fiction in this country, inhibited artistic freedom. It is an error, Howells claimed, to suppose that English and American writers have not dealt with subjects like adultery – he mentioned *The Scarlet Letter* among other examples – but they have "not made them their stock in trade; they have kept a true perspective in regard to them; they have relegated them in their pictures of life to the space and place they occupy in life itself, as we know it in England and America." Howells discouraged an American novel devoted to "guilty love" because, as he put it, "I prize fidelity in the historian of feeling and character." Infidelity as a subject for fiction, according to the "Dean" of American letters, was infidelity to the standard of nature.[16]

Edna's declaration, "I have got into a habit of expressing myself" (Chap. 36), was also her creator's. Both women insisted on their right to speak their minds about proscribed topics. By the aesthetic and moral norms of the day, both were guilty of affronting nature – Edna by her forsaking of her family, Chopin by her choice of subject. Chopin might well have contended that adultery, rather than being unnatural, was in fact far more prevalent than people like Howells suspected. But her aim in the novel is not to defend the naturalness of love outside marriage so much as it is to question the idolatry of nature. For nature is seldom an objective or neutral category: Much of what passes for the natural in a given culture's self-definition is in reality social, the social masked as the inevitable. This is particularly true in a civilization like that of the United States which prides itself on being "nature's nation." And it was never truer than in the last decades of the nineteenth century. Anti-naturalism in *fin-de-siècle* America, an America wracked by doubts about its privileged relation to nature, was a language few of Chopin's readers could have wished to hear.

4

In July 1893, less than a year before Chopin gained recognition with her first volume of tales, *Bayou Folk,* Frederick Jackson Turner delivered his famous address on "The Significance of the Frontier in American History." Turner reconceived and redirected the study of America's past by proclaiming the importance of the physical environment in shaping national character and institutions. His essay overturned the so-called germ theory of democracy, which traced popular government to its putative origins in medieval Germany. What made this country unique, Turner argued, and gave rise to individualism and nationalism as well as political liberty, was not ideas carried from Europe but the experience of settling the wilderness. The master key to United States history was the confrontation of humanity with nature: "The existence of an area of free land, its continuous recession, and the advance of American settlement westward, explain American development."[17]

Turner's interpretation at once affirmed the peculiar American bond with the natural world and commemorated its passing. He began his essay by quoting from the census report of 1890, which announced the disappearance of a moving line of settlement and thus officially marked the closing of the Western frontier. Turner was attributing national greatness to a phenomenon that no longer existed, and readers of his work could not escape the pessimistic implication that without a wilderness to sustain them, the American people faced an uncertain and difficult future. Many wondered whether the distinctive qualities of American life could survive into the next epoch. What would happen to the traits of initiative and self-reliance? Was liberty itself in danger now that it had lost its basis in nature?

Theodore Roosevelt was one of Turner's contemporaries who asked such questions, and he congratulated the historian for putting into shape "a good deal of thought which has been floating around rather loosely." The author of books on hunting, ranching, and nature observation, Roosevelt feared that the vanishing of the frontier would erode American hardihood and hasten the nation's decline into a second-class power. Contact with wild nature, he believed, was the antidote to the moral and physical softening that accompanied civilization. Roosevelt dedicated himself to revitalizing America's natural heritage. He enthusiastically promoted the cause of conservation and then, as president, established an unprecedented number of national parks and forest preserves. He also summoned his countrymen to combat mental and muscular degeneracy by spending time outdoors and leading lives of strenuous activity.[18]

Roosevelt's preoccupation with fitness and manly virtues appealed to Americans because it dovetailed with the widely held belief in the survival of the fittest, a belief that depended on an equation of nature and the human community. More than any other people in the world, Americans clung to the theories of the English sociologist Herbert Spencer, who in applying Darwin's evolutionary ideas to society gave scientific blessing to the doctrine of laissez-faire. Fidelity to Nature (invariably capitalized) was the linchpin of Spencer's philosophy. Like the physical world, the economic and social organization of humanity was a self-regulating system, governed by immutable natural laws; any attempt by government to interfere, Spencer admonished, could only have harmful consequences. Or as an American disciple, Columbia University's President Nicholas Murray Butler, put it: "Nature's cure for most social and political diseases is better than man's." To advocates of laissez-faire, the existing order was not artificial and changeable but eternal; nature authorized prevailing business

71

practices, and the economically fortunate were the products of natural selection.[19]

The paradox of laissez-faire ideology was that, rather like Turner's frontier thesis, it flourished at the very moment when it ceased to describe reality. While American businessmen were professing their faith in the naturalness of free competition, their practice was leading to consolidation and monopoly. Spencer's vogue reached its height in this country between the 1870s and the 1890s; the same years saw American economic life come under the dominance of large-scale corporations. Nature continued to exercise its hold on the native imagination even after critics began to challenge laissez-faire at the end of the century. Supporters of legislative intervention commonly made the point that regulating the trusts would restore free enterprise and permit natural law to take its course again.[20] In a further irony, the Populists of the 1890s attacked the reifying of social injustices as natural and called for welfare legislation, all the while presenting themselves as the true guardians of the natural order, people close to the land.

In literature, too, nature captured the American imagination, both as subject matter and as a model to be followed. Books about the West recorded huge sales, from Twain's *Roughing It* (1872) to Owen Wister's *The Virginian* (1903); nature writers like John Muir and John Burroughs attracted popular audiences with their studies of wildlife; and the naturalistic novelists Stephen Crane, Frank Norris, and Jack London wrote fiction celebrating the Darwinian struggle for existence. Twain poked fun at earlier romantic pictures of human interaction with the natural surroundings, most amusingly in his essay on "Fenimore Cooper's Literary Offenses" (1895). Twain took it for granted that the realist ideal of verisimilitude was valid for all literature and roundly criticized Cooper for producing work that "has no lifelikeness, . . . no seeming of reality." If the author of the Leatherstocking Tales "had any real knowledge of Nature's way of doing things," Twain complained, "he had a most delicate art in concealing the fact."[21] Twain's admirer and fellow realist, Howells, shared his conviction that the novel as a genre had matured since its romantic origins. The realist credo, he agreed, was applicable to any work of art: "Now we are beginning to see and to say that no author is an authority except in those moments when he held his ear close to Nature's lips and caught her very accent."[22]

Dissent from this veneration of nature was rare in the United States, even among those who wished to challenge the status quo. One group forced to address the issue was the women's movement, since any questioning of current gender arrangements was certain to be condemned as unnatural. Charlotte Perkins Gilman felt obliged to begin her investigation of *Women and Economics* (1898) with the argument that the human female's dependence on the male for food has no parallel among other animal species. Gilman pointed out that "the facts of life as we find them" are in many cases neither natural nor immutable, merely so familiar that we "fail to notice them" and so allow them to persist despite their causing more harm than good. A minor illustration would be the wearing of corsets, a weightier one the reduction of middle-class wives to nonproductive consumers. Gilman moved from disputing the naturalization of social customs to raising doubts about the authority of nature itself. That a given condition is "natural," she noted, doesn't necessarily make it either right or advantageous to humanity. She asked her readers to imagine, "by sheer muscular effort as it were," alternatives to such accepted usages as mothers providing the exclusive care for their young. "If it can be shown that human progress is better served by other methods, then other methods will be proven right; and we must grow to enjoy and honor them as fast as we can, and in due course of time we shall find them natural." The effect of Gilman's reasoning was to put nature as a category into question; if societies could both depart from and create the natural, the term had no absolute meaning so far as humans were concerned.[23]

Chopin was not an activist, and the bleak outcome of her novel reveals little faith in the prospect of social transformation. Yet she was as committed as Gilman to scrutinizing the claims made in the name of the natural, whether in society or in art. Dr. Mandelet, it will be recalled, spoke of the illusions fostered by nature and reinforced by culture; what Chopin sets out to show is that "the facts of life as we find them" are themselves problematic. In the aesthetic sphere, she subverts the assumption that the sign exists in a state of dependence or inferiority with regard to the thing it represents and increases in value the more closely it resembles that original reality. Unmasking both reality and realism as conventions, Chopin joins Edna in affirming self-expression. She seeks to capture in her prose the iterative, nonrepresentational character of music and to create a fiction that approximates poetry, the literary genre most akin to music in its expressiveness and self-referentiality.

5

As its title suggests, *The Awakening* is a book about sleep and dreams and their relation to reality, and like many other fictional works of the late nineteenth century it reverses the customary exaltation of the real at the expense of the imaginary. At the outset of the narrative, Edna accepts Victorian middle-class convention as the only possible form of social existence. Abjuring her girlish infatuations with a cavalry officer and a tragedian, she adopts a "realistic" attitude toward her life in consenting to marry Leonce Pontellier. "As the devoted wife of a man who worshiped her, she felt she would take her place with a certain dignity in the world of reality, closing the portals forever behind her upon the realm of romance and dreams" (Chap. 7). At this stage, Edna's "realism" is the everyday kind that bows to the way things are and regards change as remote, if not unthinkable.[24] Even after she meets Robert at Grand Isle, she continues to think of married life as synonymous with "the realities" (Chap. 7), and she initially views her attraction to the young man as "a delicious, grotesque, impossible dream" (Chap. 11).

Chopin leaves no doubt that the identification of matrimony with reality, and of fantasies or longings with unattainable dreams, is a social construct and not the irrefutable truth Edna takes it to be. Marriages like the heroine's, she writes, are accidents that "masquerade as the decrees of Fate" (Chap. 7). The novel systematically undercuts the dismissal of dreams as unreal, indicating that they may be truer revelations of the self than the procedures of the leisure class. Once Edna begins to awaken, she spends a good deal of time sleeping and dreaming: "She discovered many a

74

sunny, sleepy corner, fashioned to dream in. And she found it good to dream and be alone and unmolested" (Chap. 19). Edna's penchant for dreaming affords her access to buried desires and is a reminder of the era's interest in interior states; her history coincides with William James's experiments in psychology, Freud's early writings on dreams and the unconscious, and growing sophistication in understanding the human mind.[25] The first time she swims alone in the Gulf "is like a night in a dream," she muses to Robert (Chap. 10), and her consciousness of herself as an individual emerges out of such moments of dreaming. By the end of the book, she has turned accepted wisdom on its head and come to see "the realities" of marriage and motherhood as dreams from which she has awakened. "It was you who awoke me last summer out of a life-long, stupid dream" she tells Robert (Chap. 36), and to Dr. Mandelet she says, "it is better to wake up after all, even to suffer, rather than to remain a dupe to illusions all one's life" (Chap. 38). The existing state of affairs, in short, is no more real than the needs of one's innermost being; though too firmly entrenched for Edna to change, it need not foreclose the possibility of alternative realities.

Chopin's revision of the typical dream/reality opposition brings to mind another interest of the period: the construction in literature of ideal worlds. The device of awakening from the falsity of the present into a visionary reality is a staple of utopian fiction, more than a hundred examples of which were published in this country between the late 1880s and 1910.[26] Like Chopin's narrative, these works contest the real by exposing it as a convention; they go on to maintain that their images of the future, a time of mechanical wonders, material abundance, and social brotherhood, can be made actuality. Perhaps the most famous American utopian novel, Edward Bellamy's *Looking Backward* (1888), might plausibly have been entitled *The Awakening*. The hero, Julian West, sleeps for more than a century, from 1887 to the year 2000, and awakens in a world without injustice or want. According to Bellamy, the reality of nineteenth-century America has been an "evil dream," and West's dream of a perfect future is "this fair reality."[27] Another utopian novel redefining the relation between dream and reality is called *The Great Awakening;* published in the same year as Chopin's book, it chronicles the experiences of a man who dies in 1901 and is reincarnated in the twenty-second century. In retrospect, he tells the reader, the present world "seems but a distressing dream."[28] Turn-of-the-century utopian fantasy occurs together with and complements the realist project in American culture. Where realism denotes reality and the artist's role in reproducing it, utopianism resists the realist closure and documents the feasibility of other methods of organizing social existence. Occasionally the same authors wrote both kinds of fiction, copying nature in one work and contraverting it in a second. Howells himself composed two utopian romances, *A Traveler from Altruria* (1894) and its sequel, *Through the Eye of the Needle* (1907).[29]

The corollary to Chopin's querying of external reality is her skepticism about the dogma of representation. In her case, realism as a doctrine in literature and painting collapses along with realism as an attitude toward life. For if the real is an artifice, does it not forfeit its supposed primacy as the goal and standard of art? Numerous scenes involving efforts to render experience in words or in paint cast doubt upon the subordination of the sign to the referent. When Edna's father visits from Kentucky, and she sketches him in her studio, Chopin emphasizes the contrivance and unreality of what is being represented. The colonel sits "rigid and unflinching" before Edna's pencil, and he wears a padded coat, "which gave a fictitious breadth and depth to his shoulders and chest" (Chap. 23). Far from urging that art should imitate an original and greater reality, the tableau suggests that the subject of art, as Twain said of Cooper, is itself deficient in "lifelikeness." A similar moment occurs during Edna's dinner party when someone lays a garland of roses on Victor Lebrun's head. The young man is physically posed to create "a vision of Oriental beauty"; a white silken scarf draped over his shoulders adds "one more touch . . . to the picture." As the guests marvel at his exotic appearance, the journalist, Miss Mayblunt, exclaims, "Oh! to be able to paint in color rather than in words!" (Chap. 30). Whatever the medium used to portray him, the result would be the representation of a fiction. Or one might say that art is the image of an image, as when Edna plans a painting of Arobin and keeps a photograph from which to make a sketch of his head (Chap. 33).

Moreover, the artistic image frequently reflects something in the creator's mind and not in the physical world; it may owe its inspiration to a dream or a state of feeling. The evening Dr. Mandelet dines at the Pontelliers, Edna entertains the guests with a graphic story about a pair of lovers who ran off together to tropic islands and disappeared. So vivid is her account that it seems, in a triumph of representational art, to achieve the immediacy of reality. The listeners "could feel the hot breath of the Southern night; they could hear the long sweep of the pirogue through the glistening moonlit water . . . ; they could see the faces of the lovers, pale, close together, . . . drifting into the unknown." Although Edna's story is extraordinarily lifelike, the persons and events she describes never existed save in her imagination. "It was a pure invention. She said that Madame Antoine had related it to her. That, also, was an invention. Perhaps it was a dream she had had. But every glowing word seemed real to those who listened." As the knowing physician intuitively understands, Edna's narrative expresses the secrets of her individuality. The only reality to which it refers is the unfolding of her "inner life" (Chap. 23).

Beyond imagery, beyond representation, there is escape from natural objects altogether, a liberation that the nineteenth century tended to associate with music.[30] As Chopin's challenge to realist art is the literary analogue to Edna's rejection of Creole marriage, so her fascination with music is the aesthetic equivalent of the heroine's evolving dedication to self-expression. Chopin uses an early scene at Grand Isle to differentiate the image-free power of music from the representational ideology identified with Adele. Edna, who is "very fond of music," enjoys listening to Madame Ratignolle play the piano. "Musical strains, well rendered, had a way of evoking pictures in her mind." Adele's rendition of a piece Edna calls "Solitude" causes her imagination to summon up "the figure of a man standing beside a desolate rock on the seashore"; other pieces make her picture frolicking children and a lady caressing a cat (Chap. 9). But not long after she begins to awaken, Edna attends a musical soiree at the Lebruns and hears Mademoiselle Reisz, a true "artist at the piano," perform a Chopin prelude; this time the music stirs her emotions without representing anything:

> She waited for the material pictures which she thought would gather and blaze before her imagination. She waited in vain. She saw no pictures of solitude, of hope, of longing, or of despair. But the very passions themselves were aroused within her soul, swaying it, lashing it, as the waves daily beat upon her splendid body. She trembled, she was choking, and the tears blinded her. (Chap. 9)

An imageless art is autonomous, neither mirroring nor duplicating an external form, and it shakes Edna to the depths because it provides immediate entrance to the subjective world of feelings.

Music, then, is the artistic opposite of the Creole wife, that dependent creature who faithfully replicates her spouse. For Edna, it becomes associated with her attachment to Robert and the awakening of her independent emotional life. As a young woman, she had treasured a photograph of a great tragic actor and "dwelt upon the fidelity of the likeness" (Chap. 7). But now, as she renounces imitation as a model of behavior, she cherishes the nonrepresentational art form of music for its capacity to bring back Robert's memory and reanimate the intense sensations of their time together. On their outing to the Chenière Caminada, Robert sang an air with the recurring line, "Ah! *Si tu savais*," and Edna often hums the song in his absence, his "voice, the notes, the whole refrain haunt[ing] her memory" (Chap. 14). She also searches out and regularly visits Mademoiselle Reisz at her apartment, where she listens enraptured to a Chopin Impromptu, Robert's favorite, and breaks into sobs, as she had at Grand Isle, "when strange, new voices awoke in her" (Chap. 21). She is at Mademoiselle Reisz's waiting for the pianist and idly picking out a tune on the piano when she and Robert meet again for the first time after his return to New Orleans.

Although Robert ends up disappointing her, Edna's refusal to retreat from the objective of personal fulfillment, her insistence on expressing or reflecting no one but herself, aligns her awakening with music's apparent self-sufficiency and points toward the abstraction of modernist art. There are muted hints that in her painting the heroine tries to achieve something more expressive and subjective than the photographic likeness she used to admire. She can afford to move from her husband's house because her sketches begin to sell; her agent praises the new work for its growth "in force and individuality" (Chap. 26). One even has a sense that her painting becomes less tied to natural appearances. The last canvas she executes during the story is "a young Italian character study," and Chopin notes that she applied herself to it "all the morning, completing the work without the model" (Chap. 33).

Chopin, for her part, gravitates toward a literary art that approaches the condition both of poetry and of music. She takes as artistic models not other prose writers but a composer and a poet: Frédéric Chopin, whose preludes nurture Edna's awakening, and Walt Whitman, whose themes and sound patterns pervade the novel. The heroine's growth into awareness has been a prose "Song of Myself," resembling Whitman's poem in its preoccupation with self and candor about sexuality; and the book's final pages in particular evoke "Out of the Cradle Endlessly Rocking" in their verbal music as well as their intermingling of eros, death, and the sea.[31] Although poetry, unlike instrumental music, relies on language, it gives more weight than prose to linguistic elements that go beyond representation or communication, such as rhythms and emotive effects.[32] Even in the case of free verse, poetry tends to be more patterned, artificial, and self-referential than prose narrative, especially realist narrative that effaces itself and tries to provide an objective transcription of the actual. Chopin experiments with a lyrical, iterative style that emulates music in its attempt to surpass external reference and to highlight its own artful design. The recurrent evocations of the sea, the ominous woman in black, seemingly always dogging the unnamed pair of lovers, the symbolic birds that frame and comment on Edna's career – in these and other examples of heightened poetic effect, Chopin's writing turns inward and makes the internal life of the text its primary focus. It directs attention not just toward the objects described but also, and more importantly, toward earlier or later moments in the narrative. The novel becomes highly self-referential as it repeats phrases, incidents, and motifs in the manner of a musical composition.[33]

This self-conscious patterning is most pronounced in the last chapter, in which Edna returns to Grand Isle and the Gulf. Like a climactic refrain, the ending looks back to and stresses what has gone before: The bird fluttering down to the water recalls Edna's several exchanges with Mademoiselle Reisz about the artist "that would soar above the level plain of tradition and prejudice" (Chap. 27); Edna remembers the bluegrass meadow she walked through as a girl and reminisced about to Adele; she repeats to herself Robert's parting message, "Good-by — because I love you" (Chap. 39); and Chopin echoes her own descriptions of the sensuous touch and sonorous tone of the sea, its voice "never ceasing, whispering, clamoring, murmuring, inviting the soul to wander in abysses of solitude" (Chaps. 6, 39). Rhythmic, repetitive, sending the reader back to earlier passages, Chopin's prose at the end of *The Awakening* aspires to the self-expressiveness she identifies with her iconoclastic heroine and with music.

The conclusion of *The Awakening* also sends us back to Chopin's beginning as a fiction writer, for her commitment to music as a self-expressive art spanned her creative life; it appears in one of the very first stories she published, "Wiser Than a God" (1889). The story concerns a young woman, Paula Von Stoltz, who refuses an offer of marriage in order to fulfill herself as a musician. To the man who wishes her to become a conventional wife and mother, Paula declares that music is "something dearer than life, than riches, even than love." She goes on to attain fame and financial independence in a successful career as a concert pianist.[34] The fusion of music with self-reliant individuality realized by the heroine of this early tale haunts *The Awakening* and its narrative technique. The musiclike quality of the novel asserts that, much like Edna Pontellier, literary art exists in its own right and not simply as an image of something else.

It would be an error, however, to overstate the "modernism" of either Chopin's fiction or Edna's awakened consciousness. Neither author nor character finally manages to break free from imitative attitudes. Indeed, the very strategies the two women use to achieve autonomy are what implicate them in the value systems they oppose. Chopin's adoption of a musical style, instead of carrying her beyond imitation, discloses the extent to which her thought remains tethered to nature and committed to parroting as an aesthetic ideal. And Edna's discovery of her suppressed being, a discovery pitting her against her culture's celebration of fidelity, in all the senses of that word, unfolds as a process of shedding social conventions and becoming "like" herself, the authentic Edna Pontellier.

6

The rhythms at the end of *The Awakening,* like those in Whitman's "Out of the Cradle Endlessly Rocking," are verbal approximations of the sounds of the sea. Chopin lets the voice of the Gulf speak through her prose. Successive participles — "never ceasing, whispering, clamoring, murmuring, inviting the soul to wander in abysses of solitude" — convey the gently rocking motion of the waves. Thematically, the sea is linked to music through Edna's experience of independence as a swimmer; both music and swimming validate the heroine's rejection of a secondary or reflective role. In the passage on music's imageless power, Chopin compares the passions aroused for Edna by Mademoiselle Reisz's playing to the waves daily beating upon her body. But as this example suggests, Chopin's musical prose is in fact neither image free nor unconstrained by external reference; its iterative rhythms call to mind pictures of the sea. The effort to circumvent representation and to fashion a self-expressive narrative results in a variant of the realist project: the imitation, not of natural forms, but of natural sounds. Music also bears a mimetic relation to the songs of birds, and the concentrated repetitions at the book's close are a final reminder of the green and yellow parrot that inaugurates Edna's story by "repeating over and over" an exclamation in French (Chap. 1). Like Howells's exemplary realist author, Chopin holds her ear close to nature's lips and catches its very accent.[35]

Chopin's failure to transcend imitation through music is unsurprising: In 1899 music itself was not yet modern in the sense of being essentially inward and self-reflexive. The perception of music as a purely expressive art form was held by writers and painters rather than musicians. Music has a history like other arts, and in the nineteenth century it adhered to standardized harmonic and

81

formal principles. Not until technical changes wrought in the new century by composers like Debussy, Bartók, and particularly Schoenberg, who broke with traditional tonality, did music develop into a language that nobody understood.[36] Before the modernist revolution, program music was commonplace, and most composers had no compunction about "copying" nature in their work. One of Debussy's best-known pieces, *Le Mer*, faithfully imitates the rhythms of the sea. To Charles Ives, the most important American composer of the late Victorian period, music was always inspired by images. "Is not all music program music?" Ives asked rhetorically in the prologue to his Concord Sonata. "Is not pure music, so called, representative in its essence?"[37]

Representational or realist assumptions also color Chopin's understanding of the self and shape Edna's drive to realize her true nature. Even as a child, the heroine is said to have known "the dual life – that outward life which conforms, the inward life which questions" (Chap. 7). Edna's secret life is, of course, the "real" one, the crux of her uniqueness as a human being, and as she responds to its urgent demands, she begins to discard the "false" self she has always presented to her family and friends. Chopin writes that "she was becoming herself and daily casting aside that fictitious self which we assume like a garment with which to appear before the world" (Chap. 19). The awakened Edna ceases to comply with others' expectations and follows the promptings of her own nature, and Chopin describes this change as a growth in the heroine's authenticity, her reality, as a person. "Every step which she took toward relieving herself from obligations added to her strength and expansion as an individual. She began to look with her own eyes; to see and to apprehend the deeper undercurrents of life. No longer was she content to 'feed upon opinion' when her own soul had invited her" (Chap. 32).

By the end of the narrative, Edna has become one with the inner life that is her real identity. She commits suicide rather than continue what she now recognizes to have been a sham existence. Her gesture of casting off her garments on the beach at Grand Isle encapsulates her expulsion from her being of all inauthentic elements. Edna transposes into a personal key the realist injunction to be faithful to the actual: She makes her outward character the likeness of her private, "real" nature. Indeed, the notion that it is possible to be "like" or "unlike" oneself occurs frequently in the novel. When Robert abruptly decides to leave for Mexico, Edna exclaims to herself, "How unlike Robert!" (Chap. 15). And when Leonce Pontellier feels that his wife is behaving unpredictably, he observes to Dr. Mandelet, "She's odd, she's not like herself" (Chap. 22). Leonce is plainly mistaken; Edna has never been more integrated as a person, more in touch with her own identity. Genuine individuality in *The Awakening* is predicated on the same representational outlook that supports Creole marriage and realist art: It consists in being like oneself. Neither the heroine nor her creator is capable of imagining an awakened self liberated from mimetic consistency.

For all their unconventionality, then, Kate Chopin and Edna Pontellier retain their culture's deference to nature and the real. They have no inkling of the decentered, internally conflicted self made familiar in the twentieth century by Freud. Edna is trapped not solely by circumstances but also by her own unconscious consent to the values of her society. One could mention other examples of her allegiance to *fin-de-siècle* beliefs: Her resolve "never again to belong to another than herself" (Chap. 26) reflects the creed of possessive individualism that identifies freedom with ownership of the self and has long relegated women to an inferior position. Her statements to Dr. Mandelet, "I want to be let alone", and "I don't want anything but my own way" (Chap. 38), might have been uttered by a late-nineteenth-century entrepreneur in favor of laissez-faire economics. Perhaps Edna is doing no more than claiming for women the rights always enjoyed by men. But surely one supposition Chopin's novel obligates us to question is that women should aspire to be "like" anyone, least of all those who uphold the status quo.

It seems unfair to conclude by dwelling upon the limitations of *The Awakening* rather than its considerable achievements, specifically those qualities that enable it to rise above its historical moment and speak so forcefully to the present. Chopin's book has emerged from obscurity to "classic" status in part because it broaches themes subsequently taken up by twentieth-century feminism. *The Awakening* also remains alive because it attempts to make sense of two enigmas, nature and the self, that continue to challenge and frustrate modern understanding. I have indicated the internal contradictions in Chopin's handling of these problems, but it needs to be acknowledged that we come no closer to comprehending them today than she did nearly a hundred years ago. Does nature have objective meaning or is it always a social construct? Is it knowable or necessarily mystified by ideological pressures and the inherent inadequacies of language? Similarly, is the self accessible to understanding and definition? Does being like oneself constitute true individuality or being in contradiction with oneself? Merely to pose these questions is to reveal the persistence of confusions in our thinking about them. Perhaps it is best to conclude that the modernism of Chopin's narrative lies in her failure to provide coherent solutions to dilemmas that the twentieth century has found to be insoluble.

NOTES

1. A good survey of these developments is John Higham, "The Reorientation of American Culture in the 1890's," in *The Origins of Modern Consciousness*, ed. John Weiss (Detroit: Wayne State University Press, 1965), pp. 25–48. On the universal tendency to identify women with nature, see Sherry B. Ortner, "Is Female to Male as Nature Is to Culture?" in *Woman, Culture, and Society*, ed. Michelle Zimbalist Rosaldo and Louise Lamphere (Stanford, Calif.: Stanford University Press, 1974), pp. 67–87.

2. William Dean Howells, *Criticism and Fiction* (New York: Harper and Brothers, 1891), p. 10.

3. Ibid., pp. 26–7.

4. James D. Hart, *The Popular Book: A History of America's Literary Taste* (New York: Oxford University Press, 1950), pp. 163–8. Among other examples, Hart mentions *In His Steps* (1896) by Charles M. Sheldon, *Quo Vadis?* (1896) by Henryk Sienkiewicz, and *The Christian* (1897) by Caine Hall.

5. Charlotte Perkins Gilman, *Women and Economics: The Economic Factor Between Men and Women as a Factor in Social Evolution*, ed. Carl N. Degler (1898; rpt. New York: Harper Torchbooks, 1966), pp. 191–2, 200.

6. On the deletion of feminine physicality in Victorian literature, see Helena R. Michie, *The Flesh Made Word: Representations of Women's Bodies from the Victorian Era to the Present* (New York: Oxford University Press, 1986).

7. Meyer Schapiro, *Modern Art: Nineteenth and Twentieth Centuries: Selected Papers* (New York: George Braziller, 1982), p. 192.

8. Ibid., pp. 190–5; the quotation appears on p. 192. See also Arnold Hauser, *The Social History of Art*, 4 vols., trans. Stanley Godman (New York: Vintage Books, n.d.), Vol. 4, pp. 166–70.

9. Cézanne is quoted in James Nagel, *Stephen Crane and Literary Impressionism* (University Park: Pennsylvania State University Press, 1980), p. 12.

10. Schapiro, *Modern Art*, pp. 186–7.

11. Per Seyersted, *Kate Chopin: A Critical Biography* (Baton Rouge: Louisiana State University Press, 1969), p. 159.

12. Before her marriage, Edna conceived an adolescent infatuation for a tragedian whose framed photograph she used to kiss. I suggest subsequently that she outgrows her fondness for photographic likeness when she begins to awaken.

13. See the contemporary reviews reprinted in the Norton Critical Edition of *The Awakening*, ed. Margaret Culley (New York: Norton, 1976), pp. 145–55, especially 145–6 (the review from *The Mirror* for May 4, 1899).

14. Seyersted, *Kate Chopin*, pp. 82–4.

15. Wharton's review from the Pittsburgh *Leader* (July 8, 1899) is reprinted in the Norton Critical Edition of *The Awakening*, pp. 153–5; the quotation is from p. 154.

16. Howells, *Criticism and Fiction*, pp. 153–7.

17. Frederick Jackson Turner, "The Significance of the Frontier in American History," in *Frontier and Section: Selected Essays of Frederick Jackson Turner*, ed. Ray Allen Billington (Englewood Cliffs, N.J.: Prentice-Hall, 1961), p. 37. See also Richard Hofstadter, *The Progressive Historians: Turner, Beard, Parrington* (New York: Vintage Books, 1970), pp. 47–164.

18. On Roosevelt and conservation, see Roderick Nash, *Wilderness and the American Mind* (New Haven, Conn.: Yale University Press, 1967), pp. 149–51; and William Henry Harbaugh, *Power and Responsibility: The Life and Times of Theodore Roosevelt* (New York: Farrar, Straus and Cudahy, 1961), pp. 318–36.

19. A useful summary of laissez-faire thought in America is Max Lerner, "The Triumph of Laissez-Faire," in *Paths of American Thought*, ed.

Arthur M. Schlesinger, Jr., and Morton White (Boston: Houghton Mifflin, 1963), pp. 147–66. See also Thomas C. Cochran and William Miller, *The Age of Enterprise: A Social History of Industrial America*, 2nd ed. (New York: Harper Torchbooks, 1961), pp. 119–28; Butler is quoted on p. 126.

20. See Lerner, "The Triumph of Laissez-Faire," pp. 147–50, 157; and Harold U. Faulkner, *The Decline of Laissez-Faire, 1897–1917* (New York: Holt, Rinehart & Winston, 1951), pp. 366–82 passim.

21. Mark Twain, "Fenimore Cooper's Literary Offenses," in *The Complete Humorous Sketches and Tales of Mark Twain*, ed. Charles Neider (Garden City, N.Y.: Doubleday, 1961), pp. 642, 634.

22. Howells, *Criticism and Fiction*, p. 14.

23. Gilman, *Women and Economics*, pp. 5–6, 32, 77, 209–12.

24. On the everyday meaning of "realistic" as practical or commonsensical, see Raymond Williams, *Keywords: A Vocabulary of Culture and Society* (New York: Oxford University Press, 1976), pp. 217–18.

25. For a very different interpretation of Edna's sleeping as evidence of regression, see Cynthia Griffin Wolff, "Thanatos and Eros: Kate Chopin's *The Awakening*," *American Quarterly* 25 (1973):449–71.

26. The figures are from Neil Harris, "Utopian Fiction and Its Discontents," in *Uprooted Americans: Essays to Honor Oscar Handlin*, ed. Richard L. Bushman et al. (Boston: Little, Brown, 1979), p. 216. See also Vernon Louis Parrington, Jr., *American Dreams: A Study of American Utopias*, 2nd ed. (New York: Russell and Russell, 1964).

27. Edward Bellamy, *Looking Backward, 2000–1887*, ed. Cecelia Tichi (1888; rpt. New York: Penguin, 1982), p. 230 passim.

28. Albert Adams Merrill, *The Great Awakening: The Story of the Twenty-Second Century* (Boston: George Book Publishing Co., 1899), p. 340 passim.

29. Howells doubtless would maintain that realism is a more radical aesthetic than it appears from this analysis. Certainly a case can be made that realist art, by demystifying the way things are, actively furthers the utopian project.

30. On the nineteenth-century view of music, see Robert P. Morgan, "Secret Languages: The Roots of Musical Modernism," *Critical Inquiry* 10 (March 1984):442–7.

31. Whitman's influence on Chopin is examined by Elizabeth Balkman House, "*The Awakening*: Kate Chopin's 'Endlessly Rocking' Cycle," *Ball State University Forum* 20 (1979):53–8; and Lewis Leary, *Southern Excursions: Essays on Mark Twain and Others* (Baton Rouge: Louisiana State University Press, 1971), pp. 169–74. A relevant and suggestive

discussion of Whitman's interest in music's self-referentiality appears in John T. Irwin, *American Hieroglyphics: The Symbol of the Egyptian Hieroglyphics in the American Renaissance* (New Haven, Conn.: Yale University Press, 1980), pp. 20–40.

32. See Anthony Easthope, *Poetry as Discourse* (London and New York: Methuen, 1983), pp. 15–16 passim.

33. Lewis Leary comments about Chopin's novel: "Almost every incident or reference in *The Awakening* anticipates an incident or reference that follows it or will remind a reader of something that has happened before" (*Southern Excursions*, p. 172).

34. Kate Chopin, "Wiser Than a God," in *The Complete Works of Kate Chopin*, 2 vols., ed. Per Seyersted (Baton Rouge: Louisiana State University Press, 1969), Vol. 1, pp. 39–47; quotation is from p. 46.

35. One might also note that Chopin's philosophical outlook remains naturalist in some respects despite her quarrel with nature as a normative category. Like her contemporaries, Frank Norris and Jack London, she sees the individual as succumbing, if not to biological determinism, at least to basic instinctual urges too powerful to control.

36. This account of music's history is based on Morgan, "Secret Languages," pp. 447–61.

37. Charles Ives, *Essays Before a Sonata and Other Writings*, ed. Howard Boatwright (New York: Norton, 1962), pp. 4–7; quotation is from p. 4.

4

The Half-Life of Edna Pontellier

ANDREW DELBANCO

It was then that a new note separated itself jarringly from the soft
crying of the night . . . the noise of a woman's laughter. It began low,
incessant . . . [then] reached a high point, tensed and stifled, almost
the quality of a scream – then it ceased and left behind it a silence
empty and menacing as the greater silence overhead. . . . The room
had grown smothery. He wanted to be out in some cool and bitter
breeze, miles above the cities, and to live serene and detached back in
the corners of his mind. Life was that sound out there, that ghastly
reiterated female sound.
  – F. Scott Fitzgerald, *The Beautiful and the Damned* (1922)

1

IT is perhaps excusable to recall with a touch of envy the time
when a teacher could, without embarrassment, distribute *The
Lifetime Reading Plan* or some such guide to literacy, and expect
students to measure their progress toward adulthood by the
number of checks beside the titles read. There is a certain comfort
in the authority of lists. But, however reluctantly, one must con-
cede that it is a better measure of maturity (in a teacher as well as a
student) to know that we shall not soon have such lists again. The
idea of the classic, if it is to be saved at all in our relativistic time,
seems to need continual rescue from the idea of the absolute.
Frank Kermode, for instance, in a charming rescue operation con-
ducted about a decade ago, rested his case with this attenuated
formula: "A classic . . . is a book that is read a long time after it
was written."[1]

It is now nearly ninety years since *The Awakening* was written,
and more people are reading it than ever before. This is as it should
be. It is one of those rare books of passion managed with precision;

a virtuoso piece of formal sophistication that is also a cry from the heart. Its reputation has fluctuated – from scandal when it was published in 1899 and angrily received as an American *Madame Bovary*, to near-oblivion during the first half of this century until Cyrille Arnavon translated it into French and Robert Cantwell and Edmund Wilson began to reclaim it for our own literature. Today it can be read in any of sixteen editions. During its long dormancy *The Awakening* did manage to survive in scholarly histories and bibliographies as an example of "local color," a kind of ancillary text to the sociological study of Louisiana Creole life. But since it began its return to prominence, a great deal has changed in the conditions that make for literary reception.

For one thing, the very idea of "local color" – a phrase that cannot escape its pejorative hint of provincialism – has lately attracted new interest under the more acceptable name of "regionalism." This revival of interest carries a certain political force, a sometimes explicit claim that since regional writing has long been excluded for ideological reasons from the canon, even "relegated to the footnotes of American literary history," its recovery serves the cause of liberation from what is frequently called "cultural hegemony." "Implicit in the concept of regionalism," writes one representative scholar, "is a revision of the accepted standard of aesthetic and cultural value."

> The belief in universals has [too long] held its own in the face of attacks by what we might collectively term regional interests: black studies and the civil rights movement, women's studies and the resurgence of feminism, American studies and a return to grass-roots politics, as well as movements for gay rights, Native American heritage, and so on. Therefore, a reevaluation of regional concepts must begin by accounting for the pervasive undermining of "local" concerns and texts by the conviction the majority of citizens in the culture share that there do indeed exist "universals."

Reclaiming the regional tradition amounts, in this view, to nothing less than an act of solidarity with the excluded, the oppressed, the "marginalized." The regional fiction of Sarah Orne Jewett, for example, is said by another critic to celebrate "a series of characters who illustrate the richness of life a woman can achieve . . .

alone." Regionalism would seem to be a literature about the heroism of those Americans who refuse assimilation.[2]

It may, however, be worth enlarging the question briefly beyond the sphere of academic literary study, if only to suggest that there is something partial about this view. As recently as twenty years ago in America, the "revision of accepted standards of cultural value" chiefly meant revision of such "universals" as these: race hatred, indifference toward the poor, and tolerance of prevailing conditions in the industrial workplace. The revision of such values was, moreover, carried out not regionally, but from the nation's center of political power as a social experiment that has been attacked ever since the post–Civil War years of Reconstruction – from the left as inadequate and cynically reformist for the purpose of defusing socially "dangerous" energies, and from the right as extravagant and antilibertarian. In what is surely a conspicuous irony, the language of antagonism toward centralized power has become the shared property of the political right and the literary left. One remembers, for instance, how often Richard Nixon invoked the formula that it was "time for power to stop flowing from the people to the capital, and to start flowing from the capital to the people." This kind of rhetoric remains dominant, obviously enough, in the politics of the eighties, and has become, in proximate form, the leading language of cultural criticism as well. Regionalism is celebrated in the leftish academy as an assault on what are often called the "norms" of American ideology – patriarchy, laissez-faire, imperial ambition, the calculated illusion of classlessness – whereas the idea of regional autonomy is invoked on the right as the restoration of American "values": local authority, individualism, enterprise free from external restraint. I would suggest that these apparently contradictory attitudes, often denoted by tonally divergent nouns such as "norm" and "value," are not as far apart as they may appear, but are in fact two forms of anti-federalism – an impulse variously on the ascendant at the present time.[3]

One reason, then, that *The Awakening* has recovered its audience may be that it expresses both these current regional impulses – the subversive and the curatorial – at once. It is a book uncomfortable, and therefore maneuverable, within ideological categories. As anyone knows who has ever discussed it in the classroom, it can be read with assent by readers of quite opposite positions on issues of sexual politics. It does lament the infiltration of middle-class "norms" into a regional enclave, but the enclave itself hardly qualifies as a haven of egalitarian or feminist principles. *The Awakening* is, in short, a book of divided loyalties toward its own subject: the collision between French Catholic culture and the American mainstream, of which Edna Pontellier – daughter of a Kentucky Presbyterian minister – is a sort of ambassador. Chopin, whose own family of O'Flahertys and Charnevilles was a living embodiment of such a collision, attempts reconciliation between these two cultures by celebrating a conservative ideal of responsible freedom that she associates specifically with two Creole women – one, Madame Ratignolle, a mother and wife; the other, Mademoiselle Reisz, an unmarried musician. If *The Awakening* begins as a critique of female domestication, it closes with an emotion that is unmistakably restorationist.

It is a book, then, that is unlikely to yield radical social doctrine. Among its demands is the imperative that we not reduce Edna Pontellier's experience to paraphrase or platitude – neither in the service of a feminist critique of patriarchal authority, nor as a reactionary denunciation of cultural change. If we would attempt to meet that demand, it is perhaps appropriate to start with the men who surround and drive her to rebellion.

2

The men of *The Awakening* are of a recognizable sort in turn-of-the-century American fiction. We know them, for instance, through Henry James: "Young men are very different from what I was," says the elder Mr. Touchett in *The Portrait of a Lady* (1884); "when I cared for a girl – when I was young – I wanted to do more than look at her." There are many echoes of that remark in the literature of the nineties: One may think not only of James's ineffectual males, but of Dreiser's Hurstwood descending through shabbiness to despair, or of Stephen Crane's "youth" trying to prove himself on the battlefield, or, a little later, of this complaint from Mrs. Bart in Edith Wharton's *The House of Mirth* (1905): "It had been among that lady's grievances that her husband [whose bankruptcy and death have left the family groping for position] — in the early days, before he was too tired — had wasted his evenings in what she vaguely described as 'reading poetry'." If we can trust the literary record, America at the turn of the century seems to have been populated by men who could not cope.

Kate Chopin agreed. She witnessed in New Orleans what Wharton saw in New York and Jewett in New England: a once haughty privileged class on the edge of extinction, nominally led by men who were in a condition too shriveled to lead. Robert Lebrun (Edna's first infatuation), for example, brings his "high voice" and "serio-comic" charm each summer to the resort at Grand Isle, where he constitutes "himself the devoted attendant of some fair dame or damsel . . . sometimes a young girl, [or] a widow . . . [or] some interesting married woman." He seems best pleased as a kind of humored troubadour sitting at the feet of an unavailable lady. From this posture he recites titillating accounts of his amorous adventures, and is excited in turn by "the lady at the needle [who] kept up a little running, contemptuous comment: *'Blagueur — farceur — gros bête, va!'* " There is a hint of sexual self-abasement here, but in the end such entertainments on even the hottest Louisiana nights feel more filial than carnal. This man has fallen out of the active world. He has become something between a jester and a gigolo.

Male attenuation is, then, one of the themes that Chopin shares with other regional writers of her time — with Jewett, for instance, whose *Country of the Pointed Firs* (1896) is populated by men who are either drifting into senility or frozen in boyhood, keeping about them "a remote and juvenile sort of silence." But it is also a theme of wider than regional concern. Where Jewett gives us a settled psychic condition as a consequence of New England's economic impoverishment, Chopin shows us a southern version of the same problem as social *process* — a process that she makes visible by giving us glimpses of Creole men in various consenting or resistant relations to it. Mr. Pontellier, for example, although he is in many ways a traditionalist and much bewildered by his wife's disregard for custom, is nevertheless engaged in certain rebellions of his own: He is, quietly and without anything like his wife's risk of shame, disowning his culture. He speaks English "with no accent whatever" (whereas the Ratignolles retain an "un-English emphasis" in their speech) and is moving cannily into the national economy – even spending the latter part of the novel offstage, on business in New York. Monsieur Ratignolle, again by contrast (he is always "Monsieur" and his wife "Madame," whereas the Pontelliers are Mr. and Mrs.), remains committed to the local and to the past. His house, which Chopin presents as a legible emblem of his identity, is "on the corner of a side street," and his domesticity is physically inseparable from his work: "his family lived in commodious apartments over the store . . . which enjoyed a steady and prosperous trade." Carrying on his father's business, Monsieur Ratignolle is the farthest thing from the *nouvel homme* that Mr. Pontellier is gingerly trying to become.

Some members of the older generation, then, are taking tentative steps out of the past, while others are digging in. But among the young men, there are fewer distinctions to be made. They are all, to put it simply, devoted to dissipation. Robert leaves for Mexico with no evident itinerary. Alcee Arobin, who has no evident vocation (except to be Edna's second and more willing conquest), admits that his name is "permitted . . . to decorate the . . . letterheads [of a New Orleans law firm] and to appear upon a shingle that graced Perdido Street." Even the street name signifies an unanchored life – a way of living with which the vulgar world is becoming less and less patient: "'There are so many inquisitive people and institutions abounding,' said Arobin, 'that one is really forced as a matter of convenience these days to assume the virtue of an occupation if he has it not.'" Those who once formed the governing class of the city are badly adrift, and Chopin surrounds them with an alien bustle.[4]

The figures who walk the line between these worlds are the Pontelliers, especially Edna. Sometimes she even follows a literal border: "I saw her," reports Doctor Mandelet, ". . . walking along Canal Street" – the avenue that separates the old city from the new. She walks suspended between a leisured culture that is dying and a business culture that is thriving; a route defined by a series of opposing architectural metaphors. Her own house, for instance, dressed and painted "a dazzling white" to please the world's scanning eye, is an expression of Creole femininity as a self-advertising bauble. Graceful, glad to be owned, its "round, fluted columns support the sloping roof." It is also, of course, Edna's prison. (Chopin confers upon her a sense of confinement from the opening detail of the caged parrot to the suffocating end.) But she occasionally gets a furlough, and the place where she most likes to spend her freed moments is the home of Mademoiselle Reisz, whose "apartments up under the roof" are high above the world of noise and barter. "There were plenty of windows in [Mademoiselle Reisz's] little front room. They were for the most part dingy, but as they were nearly always open it did not make so much difference. . . . From her windows could be seen the crescent of the river, the masts of ships and the big chimneys of the Mississippi steamers." If Edna's house is all surfaces, the home of Mademoiselle Reisz is self-sufficiently internal, yet also bravely open to the world.

Much of the novel is concerned with Edna's attempt to learn something from this example; with her struggling to open her mind to the meaning of the appurtenances – some chosen, some not – among which she must live out her life. To put it another way, Edna begins to understand that she can modify, if not transform, the scenes of her existence. Rooms, views, streets, furnishings – in the full sense of the word, *décor* – are a realm of experience whose significance had once been lost on her. Now that she begins to distinguish between the life assigned to her and the possibility of fashioning herself anew, she makes her boldest (and most often quoted) declaration: "I would give up the unessential; I would give away my money, I would give my life for my children; but I wouldn't give myself." With this series of renunciations, she has begun to sense the existence of an irreducible self. But the question is – and it becomes the novel's most urgent question – what constitutes this essential self? What can finally be discarded as "unessential"? Edna's first hint of an answer, as she rises out of the automatism of her appointed role as imported wife, is her discovery, encouraged by Madame Ratignolle in their sensual encounter on the beach, that self-awareness begins with the sense of touch:

> Edna, left alone in the little side room, loosened her clothes, removing the greater part of them. She bathed her face, her neck and arms

in the basin that stood between the windows. She took off her shoes and stockings and stretched herself in the very center of the high, white bed. How luxurious it felt to rest thus in a strange, quaint bed, with its sweet country odor of laurel lingering about the sheets and mattress! She stretched her strong limbs that ached a little. She ran her fingers through her loosened hair for a while. She looked at her round arms as she held them straight up and rubbed them one after the other, observing closely, as if it were something she saw for the first time, the fine, firm quality and texture of her flesh. She clasped her hands easily above her head, and it was thus she fell asleep. (Chap. 13)

This expression of Whitmanesque autoeroticism (we know that Chopin savored *Leaves of Grass*) is one of many reminders that she had wanted to call her novel "A Solitary Soul."[5] Edna's husband, complaining that he meets her only "at breakfast," is more mystified than pleased by her new assertion of sensual need. In Robert she encounters a still franker fear of her sexuality: "His face [grows] a little white" when she gives him a glimpse of it. Even Arobin, though less hesitant to test her desire, is more voyeur than lover. Edna, in short, is a woman in thwarted pursuit of partnership, and as her search proceeds, she is more and more infected by loneliness. Whenever she hears Mademoiselle Reisz play a certain plaintive melody (though she knows that "the name of the piece was something else") she calls it "Solitude," and imagines "the figure of a man standing [naked] beside a desolate rock on the seashore." Edna's worlds, both experienced and projected, are always dominated by a single figure interrupting an unpeopled vista. Her situation calls to mind Marilyn Monroe's rejoinder at the opening of *The Misfits*: The devastated young husband, just discarded on the courthouse steps, begs her to say what motives have led her to divorce him. "If I have to be alone," she replies, "I'd rather be by myself." Edna, no less, is surrounded by men without presence.

Yet Chopin insists – and with this insistence begins to revoke Edna's license to live entirely by her own resources – that being "by myself" is not ultimately possible. In her repudiation of the "unessential," Edna tries to free herself from what Henry James calls "the envelope of circumstances." She refuses, first of all, to be part of her husband's bric-a-brac. Yet there must come a time for substitutions, and when it comes, she begins to create an environment of her own choosing, a process that begins in earnest with Leonce's departure for New York. As the day for his leaving draws near, Edna scurries about the house in a new kind of agitation — guilty, we suspect, not so much over the fact of remaining as over her premonition about the temptations of independence. "She was solicitous about his health and his welfare. She bustled around, looking after his clothing, thinking about heavy underwear, quite as Madame Ratignolle would have done under similar circumstances." There is a disturbing poignance here: Edna, nearly twenty-nine, behaves like a child of sixteen whose conscience acts up in anticipation of a weekend without authority. But when she is at last left alone, relief conquers guilt, and she tours "her" house with a combination of proprietorship and sensory excitement:

> A feeling that was unfamiliar but very delicious came over her. She walked all through the house, from one room to another, as if inspecting it for the first time. She tried the various chairs and lounges, as if she had never sat and reclined upon them before. And she perambulated around the outside of the house, investigating, looking to see if windows and shutters were secure and in order. The flowers were like new acquaintances; she approached them in a familiar spirit, and made herself at home among them. The garden walks were damp, and Edna called to the maid to bring out her rubber sandals. And there she stayed, and stooped, digging around the plants, trimming, picking dead, dry leaves. The children's little dog came out, interfering, getting in her way. She scolded him, laughing at him, played with him. The garden smelled so good and looked so pretty in the afternoon sunlight. Edna plucked all the bright flowers she could find, and went into the house with them, she and the little dog. (Chap. 24)

This is a passage into discovery, but not, I think, an introduction to self-knowledge. Edna's mood of release at Leonce's departure, which begins as sheer exultation, quickly becomes conscious and strategic, until she takes the first real step toward remaking the context of her life. She will, she decides, move out of the big house into a cottage around the block — "Just two steps away," she tells Mademoiselle Reisz, who has challenged her for an explanation. "I'm tired of looking after that big house. It never seemed like

97

mine, anyway — like home." As Mademoiselle Reisz senses, the key word is "mine"; Edna is developing a taste for ownership.

More and more mastered by this desire, she falls into pecuniary explanation:

> Oh! I see there is no deceiving you. Then let me tell you: It is a caprice. I have a little money of my own from my mother's estate, which my father sends me by driblets. I won a large sum this winter on the races, and I am beginning to sell my sketches. (Chap. 26)

It is now possible to see why Chopin has used a teasing sentence of possible irony to mark the moment of the novel's shift from the open spaces of Grand Isle to the interiors of New Orleans: "The Pontelliers possessed a charming home on Esplanade Street." The force of this sentence, it turns out, lies in the fact that it is not ironic at all. Edna has become an equal partner in its plural subject — a possessor too. She has, in other words, begun to escape the condition of being (or at least learning to be) a Creole woman. But it is not sufficient to speak of what she has left behind. To come fully to terms with this novel, we must confront the terrible limbo into which Edna now falls. By the time of Leonce's departure, *The Awakening* has become a book about her suspension not merely between Kentucky Presbyterianism and Creole Catholicism, or between halves of the city divided by Canal Street, but between the genders themselves.

It is a transformation that has been hinted from the start. "She was rather handsome than beautiful," we are told early, and before long she learns to drink "liquor from the glass as a man would have done." This most basic of the novel's suspensions — between the feminine and the masculine as forms of social being — takes a predictably large psychic toll. Edna's statement that "I am beginning to sell my sketches," for instance, is a check on her emerging artistic commitment, which is explicitly associated with female dissent from the male world of commodity display and exchange. Surely her moment of highest self-realization comes when she is able — as no one else is save Madame Ratignolle (with her children) and Mademoiselle Reisz (with her music) — to take pleasure in the intrinsic value of something she has produced: "She had reached a stage [with her painting] where she seemed to be no longer feeling her way, working, when in the humor, with sureness and ease. And being devoid of ambition, and striving not toward accomplishment, she drew satisfaction from the work in itself." In Chopin's world, at least, this is an experience unavailable, or, more accurately, unaffordable, for men. Edna's brush with it is one of those moments when it is useful to think of *The Awakening* in roughly Marxian terms; she has done nothing less than make an escape from alienation.[6] Even if it is only a fleeting freedom, she conceives, for a moment, of neither her work nor herself as a commodity – which is why "I am beginning to sell my sketches" is double-edged. What in one sense is a tremor of professionalism – a feminist victory – is also a lapse into equating the expression of self with goods and services whose value depends on social use. Both aspects of Edna's awakening – the liberating and the constricting – are adumbrated in the brilliant account of her father's visit: Once a proud colonel in the Confederate army, now an astringent minister, he sits "before her pencil . . . rigid and unflinching, as he had faced the cannon's mouth in days gone by." This is, if ever there was one, a phallic pencil; an emblem of daughterly usurpation. As both Mademoiselle Reisz and Madame Ratignolle begin to realize, Edna is replacing her thralldom to particular men – father, husband, imagined lovers – with the thrill of partaking in exactly the experience that they had once monopolized: the experience of power.

We begin to feel that this exchange of roles creates the conditions for her self-destruction:

> "Take the fan," said Edna, offering it to [Robert].
> "Oh, no! Thank you. It does no good; you have to stop fanning some time, and feel all the more uncomfortable afterward."
> "That's one of the ridiculous things which men always say. I have never known one to speak otherwise of fanning." (Chap. 15)

Speaking here from the clarity of distance about male consciousness, Edna is able to repudiate sequence and causality as mental concerns because they have never been of any particular concern to her: "The past was nothing to her, it offered no lesson which she was willing to heed." She mocks Robert for the calculus of pain and pleasure that he applies to the most trivial choices. She has had enough of computation; enough, when she wants to linger in the night, of Leonce's "you will take cold out there." To fan or not to fan, she suggests, is a pathetic question. Edna is learning a new language of impulse that is, at least within the universe of the novel, explicitly identified as female, and this is precisely why it is so ominous when she falls back into the mimicry of men: "I hardly think we need new fixtures, Leonce. Don't let us get anything new: you are too extravagant. I don't believe you ever think of saving or putting by." Such uxorious language is a fair imitation of Leonce's nagging; Edna is wavering, insecure in her new self, beginning to notice that her new "feminine" discourse flusters the men around her. And so she relents, making her fatal compromise. The captive is learning to emulate the captor.

It should be said that Edna's "awakening" never wholly renovates her consciousness. She "never awakens," as one critic points out, "to the dimensions of her social world . . . never sees how the labor of the mulatto and black women around her makes her narcissistic existence possible."[7] Because of the servitude of others, she is able to keep the world of her children at a muted distance: "The boys were being put to bed; the patter of their bare, escaping feet could be heard occasionally, as well as the pursuing voice of the quadroon." The children's life upstairs is all very abstract to Edna, a bit of background noise. She exists in a relation to governess and children that is not very different from her husband's. Even childbirth itself is something she had once barely apprehended through an anesthetic haze. And the numbness lingers not merely as remembered therapy, but as a present stupor that, despite the novel's title (chosen, we should recall, by the publisher, not the author), closes tighter and tighter around her as her "awakening" proceeds: "She felt no interest in anything about her. The street, the children, the fruit vender, the flowers growing there under her eyes, were all part and parcel of an alien world." Sensory deprivation is another point toward which she converges in company with the men around her. Leonce, for instance, sits at their dining table, pouring "pepper, salt, vinegar, mustard — everything within reach" into his soup, fighting grimly against his own loss of sensation. He and Edna, we begin to realize, are not so much an opposition as a matched pair, a symmetry that Chopin carefully evokes

100

by balancing the opening chapter with the last: Our first sight of Leonce comes as he watches his wife emerge from the sea; we watch *with* him, feeling his isolation as she twines into intimacy with Robert beneath the "pink-lined shelter" of her sunshade; then, at the other end of the book, we watch Edna walk back into the sea and feel that first moment echoed – if reversed.

But if Edna and Leonce have descended into half-life together, there are nevertheless differences between their strategies for survival. For him the only release is to carry on his business, to make the pretense that nothing is off-center in his life. For Edna, the resort is to sex:

> She leaned over and kissed [Robert] – a soft, cool, delicate kiss, whose voluptuous sting penetrated his whole being – then she moved away from him. . . . She took his face between her hands and looked into it as if she would never withdraw her eyes more. (Chap. 36)

Granting to Edna this control over the rhythm of penetration and withdrawal, Chopin takes her still further away from "femininity." Squeamish Robert is, of course, appalled; "foolish boy," Edna calls him, and declares herself "no longer one of Mr. Pontellier's possessions. . . . I give myself where I choose." It is a gift he declines to receive.

Arobin, she finds, is more willing to parry her thrusts, and yet there is a gathering darkness about this succession of lovers. Careful to employ a language of pathology rather than of regained health, Chopin remarks that "the excitement [of Arobin's presence] came back upon her like a remittent fever." She acquaints Edna with desire – not only for men, but for drink, for gambling, for anything that will heat her blood. It is an appetite of which Edna is aware to the point of fear:

> "Will you go to the races again?" he asked.
> "No," she said. "I've had enough of the races. I don't want to lose all the money I've won, and I've got to work when the weather is bright, instead of –"
> "Yes; work; to be sure. You promised to show me your work. What morning may I come up to your atelier? To-morrow?"
> "No!"
> "Day after?"

> "No, no."
> "Oh, please don't refuse me! I know something of such things. I might help you with a stray suggestion or two."
> "No. Good night. Why don't you go after you have said good night? I don't like you," she went on in a high, excited pitch, attempting to draw away her hand. She felt that her words lacked dignity and sincerity, and she knew that he felt it. (Chap. 25)

Arobin has attached himself to her not with anything resembling love, but with an anthropological interest in a woman who has put away her husband, who paints, and who plays the horses like a man. There is something satanic in his concern; his patronizing visit to her studio would, she knows, somehow soil her. She does not want to paint for the likes of him, to be beholden to him; and as their confrontation comes to its manifold climax, she pays a very high price for her excitement:

> ". . . I can tell what manner of woman you are." His fingers strayed occasionally down to her warm, smooth cheeks and firm chin, which was growing a little full and double.
> "Oh, yes! You will tell me that I am adorable; everything that is captivating. Spare yourself the effort."
> "No; I shan't tell you anything of the sort, though I shouldn't be lying if I did."
> "Do you know Mademoiselle Reisz?" she asked irrelevantly. . . .
> "I'm told she's extremely disagreeable and unpleasant. Why have you introduced her at a moment when I desired to talk of you?" (Chap. 27)

Edna has, of course, introduced Mademoiselle Reisz not "irrelevantly" at all, but as a last shield against him. Work and sex are explicitly countervailed at this critical moment, just as they are in a number of Chopin's best stories, which document a woman's refusal to be transported out of vocation into sexual attachment.[8] Arobin, Edna knows, is nothing more than a measure of her desperation to find an antidote to numbness.

He is, however, no fool. He chides her with wicked aptness about her plan to hold a *fête* in honor of her departure from the old house: "What about the dinner," he asked, "the grand event, the *coup d'état?*" His phrasing cannot be improved upon, for it drives home the point that Edna's is to be a revolution in incidentals only. Nothing, he implies, will change except the identity of the ruler, a proposition with which Chopin appears to agree: "There was something in her attitude, in her whole appearance when she leaned her head against the high-backed chair and spread her arms, which suggested the regal woman, the one who rules, who looks on, who stands alone." With Mademoiselle Reisz propped on a cushioned chair as if in proxy for Edna's absent children, the whole affair has an air of unintentional self-mockery. It is a Creole gathering without familial cheer, a sapped generation feasting itself. Edna sits, as always, alone, presiding at a childless table while her lover undergoes interrogation by the one man present who speaks for the *ancien régime* – Monsieur Ratignolle. This is one of the great parties in American literature; it ranks with the Coreys' dinner in *The Rise of Silas Lapham*, the Touchetts' tea at Gardencourt, the revels on Gatsby's lawn. It is even, one might suggest, a harbinger of the forced *gemütlichkeit* of *Goodbye, Columbus* – except that (and the exception signals Chopin's startling modernity) the focus of attention is not on a wayward daughter, but on a married woman sitting in her husband's chair. Convened as an acknowledgement of beginnings – the move into the "pigeon house," the arrival of Edna's thirtieth year – it more truly marks her end. After this *coup d'état*, the rest of the novel is a long coda.

3

What makes the final pages of *The Awakening* so painful is their accumulating sense that Edna is living with foreknowledge of her doom. She begins to sputter in sentences that start and stall and start again: "There are periods of despondency and suffering which take possession of me," she tells Doctor Mandelet. "But I don't want anything but my own way. That is wanting a good deal, of course, when you have to trample upon the lives, the hearts, the prejudices of others – but no matter – still, I shouldn't want to trample upon the little lives. Oh! I don't know what I'm saying, Doctor. Good night. Don't blame me for anything." It was this kind of self-exoneration – what Willa Cather in her review called "unbalanced idealism" – that offended Chopin's first readers. Edna has lost a battle that, according to the respectable opinion of her time, she should never have begun. She has lost her fight against ennui, and what is worse, she knows it: "There was no one thing in the world that she desired. There was no human being whom she wanted near her except Robert; and she even realized that the day would come when he, too, and the thought of him would melt out of her existence, leaving her alone." Her walk into the sea is a deliverance from a limbo that Chopin is at pains to liken to that of the mulatto woman in whose home Edna takes her almost final refuge: "Do you come here often?" Robert asked, in Catiche's garden. "I almost live here," she answered.

This bitter remark, I would suggest, tells a great deal about what sort of book *The Awakening* finally becomes. It is a clue by which we may arrive at a sense of its genre. I have tried to indicate some of the ways in which this novel resists categorization, especially as a work of the regional imagination; and to suggest that it may be thought of as one of those books devoted to exposing the corrosive male fear of female sexuality – what Henry Adams had in mind when he remarked that "the monthly-magazine-made American female had not a feature that would have been recognized by Adam," or what Scott Fitzgerald meant to evoke when he spoke of "that ghastly reiterated female sound." It is a fear that runs deep through American culture – from *Godey's Lady's Book* to the *Playboy* airbrush – and Chopin wrote her novel in part to expose it. Such was, of course, not nearly her whole intention. (Elaine Showalter has usefully pointed to "a genre we might call the novel of the woman of thirty,"[9] to which Chopin's book may also be said to belong, as a work about obstruction in the lives of women whose major life decisions have already been made.) Bearing in mind, then, that this is a novel of many purposes, I want to propose still one more way to think about it – a way that I think is implicit in the detail of my reading. *The Awakening* is, it seems to me, an instance of what may be called the novel of "passing." I do not mean to suggest that it is somehow cryptically about a light-skinned black passing for white, but that it is about a woman passing for a man.

Since we have become accustomed to literalization in such matters, it is perhaps prudent to say that this description is meant to be understood as less than literal; as a suggestion that the psychological pressure that *The Awakening* inflicts upon its reader runs close to that of a mode of fiction that flourished around the turn of the century and took the predicament of the mulatto as its main theme. A representative example is Charles Chesnutt's *The House Behind the Cedars* (1900), a book that (typically for the genre) attacks the premises of racism (as *The Awakening* does the idea of woman's "proper place") by demonstrating the danger of revealed genealogy in a racist society: "One drop of black blood makes the whole man black," says one of the many bigots in Chesnutt's book, and we cringe – much as we do when Leonce rattles off the time-honored proscriptions that Edna is beginning to defy. Yet the suspense of Chesnutt's novel builds as the white lover stumbles close to fatal knowledge – the knowledge that there is "black blood" in the veins of his beloved. Holding our breath as we follow her efforts to conceal the "truth" from him, we become complicit in a strategy that amounts to a repudiation of her past. The meaning of blackness in such a book becomes a drifting illusion: A woman is black only if someone knows it, only if (in William Wells Brown's phrase) "the melting mezzotinto" in the iris of her eye is noticed by too shrewd a racial purist. I suspect that this reduction of black identity to an epistemological riddle goes some distance toward explaining why Chesnutt spent the last thirty years of his life in literary silence.

Except for a few stories and reviews, Chopin, too, fell silent before her writing life seemed ready to end. She was explicitly concerned with the mulatto theme only rarely, most famously in "Desiree's Baby." Yet *The Awakening,* too, can be understood as a work organized around the discrepant identities of an alien woman. It spurs us to wish Edna free; and yet, the more we share her claustrophobia and then the exhilaration of her release, the more we miss the degree to which she commits herself to learning precisely the social instincts of those who have made her an alien in the first place. Edna, in short, becomes what she once fled, just as the "ex-colored" wakes one day to find herself irredeemably white. In this sense, *The Awakening* can also be said to share some of the paradigmatic elements of the slave narrative – the most important formal precedent for the novel of passing. By this I mean to suggest that Chopin tells her story of a woman's carnal eruption not so much with sympathetic enthusiasm (as her first

105

readers charged) but rather as a cautionary tale – in much the same way that Frederick Douglass, for example, set out to shock his white audiences by hinting at the barbarism that slavery would eventually unleash in the enslaved.

I propose these parallels not as an exercise in literary affiliation, but because I believe that if we think of Chopin's novel as a relative of such works, we can more fully acknowledge majesty in Edna's recognition that her "awakening" is becoming a new form of degradation. And, most important, we may feel how insufficient is her death as an expression of a human being's need to find some third way between the alternatives of submission and emulation when faced by those who regard power as the ground of all human relations.

NOTES

1. Frank Kermode, *The Classic: Literary Images of Permanence and Change* (Cambridge, Mass.: Harvard University Press, 1983), p. 117.

2. Marjorie Pryse, "Literary Regionalism and the 'General Gender': Time, Place, Myth, and Friendship," *The Bennington Review* 16 (Spring 1984): 23; Emily Toth, Introduction to *Regionalism and the Female Imagination: A Collection of Essays* (University Park: Pennsylvania State University Press, 1985), p. 26.

3. I have tried to suggest elsewhere that literary regionalism in America has tended to express, if not conceal, a regressive politics ("The Rise and Fall of American Regionalism," *Bennington Review* 16 [Spring 1984]:75–9). For Chopin's own judgment on the regional movement, see her largely negative review of Hamlin Garland's manifesto, *Crumbling Idols* (1894), in Per Seyersted, ed., *The Complete Works of Kate Chopin* (Baton Rouge: Louisiana State University Press, 1969), pp. 693–4.

4. For an interesting account of the cultural consequences when "the old Creole city and the new Anglo-American plantation system were symbiotically joined," see James Marston Fitch, "Creole Architecture 1718–1860: The Rise and Fall of a Great Tradition," in Hodding Carter, ed., *The Past as Prelude: New Orleans, 1718–1968* (New Orleans: Tulane University Press, 1968), pp. 71–87. Chopin, whose husband's death in 1883 was preceded by his failure in business, was surely not immune to the elegiac mood toward Creole culture that grew as the

century waned; see, for example, such works of lamentation for French decline as Marc de Villiers du Terrage, *Les Dernieres Années de la Louisiane Française* (1904).

5. See Lewis Leary, "The Awakening of Kate Chopin," in his *Southern Excursions: Mark Twain and Others* (Baton Rouge: Louisiana State University Press, 1971), pp. 159–75.

6. A thoughtful discussion of the significance of work in the novel is Paula S. Berggren, " 'A Lost Soul': Work without Hope in *The Awakening*," *Regionalism and the Female Imagination* 3 (Spring 1977):1–7.

7. Elaine Showalter, "The Death of the Lady (Novelist): Wharton's *House of Mirth*," *Representations* 9 (Winter 1985):145.

8. See, for instance, "Wiser Than a God" (1889) and "Aunt Lympy's Interference" (1897).

9. Showalter, "The Death of the Lady," 133.

Edna's Wisdom: A Transitional and Numinous Merging

CRISTINA GIORCELLI

T HE human being who has a soul does not obey anyone but the universe,"[1] wrote the French poet Gabriel Germain. Readers of Kate Chopin's *The Awakening* keep asking themselves whether the protagonist, Edna Pontellier, abandoning herself to the waters of the Gulf of Mexico at the end of the book, obeys the universe and therefore the needs of her soul; or whether, "idly, aimlessly, unthinking and unguided" – as she has lived for twenty-eight years – she simply lets herself be carried into the unknown "rapt in oblivious forgetfulness." The question of whether Chopin intends Edna's disappearance to be regarded as a victory (the mythical apotheosis of her integrity, whatever its cost)[2] or a defeat (the inevitable outcome of her hubris, whatever its motivation).[3]

The ending is indeed ambiguous because it is "open" and technically "circular." We do not actually "see" Edna drown but see her instead surrounded by and bathed in symbols of fertility and immortality (the sea, the sun, bees). To this extent, the ending is open. At the same time, it is technically circular because the narrative movement in the last chapter reverts to the very beginning of the book, which is set on the sensuous, promising Gulf of Mexico. The close thus presents an equivocal "solution." There is the implied suicide, but Edna may have begun to live at another level of existence.

Since the critical discovery of the book in the 1960s, the elusiveness of its ending and the puzzling treatment of its protagonist's personality have caused critics to examine it mainly from two stances. From a feminist point of view, Edna's plight is that of a woman who finally begins "to realize her position in the universe as a human being, and to recognize her relations as an individual to the world within and about her." Although her spiritual and social quest is not represented as successful,[4] it is regarded as attesting to the New Woman's awareness of her right to be herself and even, when necessary, to take her own life as the ultimate statement of self-assertion. From the point of view of stylistic coherence,[5] however, the message of *The Awakening* is blurred by the dichotomies and ambiguities that pervade the entire narration. The author's wavering hold on surface and underlying meanings, ironic and serious tones, direct and indirect statements indicates a refusal to take sides and baffles judgment.

The Awakening escapes basic, clear-cut definitions from the viewpoint of both its technique and its theoretical allegiance to one or another literary mode (realism, naturalism, symbolism). Is it a novel or an extended short story? Does Chopin intend to deal with the spiritual growth and deep transformation of her protagonist, or does she intend to disclose the pitiful fatuity and inevitable failure of human aspirations? With regard to the more technical problem, the main character is psychologically, emotionally, and socially drawn in terms so stark as almost to oversimplify her case. Moreover, information about the other characters or the background situation is presented in an apparently casual and indefinite manner. As far as the more theoretical purposes are concerned, rather than either turning into a socially accepted self or helplessly suffering the insults of malevolent chance, Edna is steeped in ontological ambivalence. She seems only intermittently to be able to take a firm grasp of the world. If at times "she felt as if a mist had been lifted from her eyes, enabling her to look upon and comprehend the significance of life, that monster made up of beauty and brutality," at other times she is confused and hesitant. She muses, "if one might go on sleeping and dreaming – but to wake up and find – oh! well! perhaps it is better to wake up after all, even to suffer, rather than to remain a dupe to illusions all one's life."

The book's meaning and structure may be better recognized and valued if one takes a many-sided perspective and allows a number of options to coexist and play off against one another. Such a reading does not choose between or reconcile dualities, but holds

110

them in what Richard Wilbur, in another context, calls "honed abeyance." The conclusion would then acquire another, further significance. If the open and circular ending eludes our expectations as to the meaning of Edna's final plunge, it might be seen as purposely flexible. Chopin matches the structure with the thematic content of the book: a cyclical view of existence.

The complex and composite subject presented in the narrative is appropriately introduced by the linguistic features of its title.[6] Syntactically, as it consists of an *-ing* clause, it is a blend of nominal *and* verbal functions. Semantically, it designates a border condition that, while linking two (or three) opposing ones (sleeping and/or dreaming versus waking up), partakes of both and points to a form of semisomnambulism, to living and acting in the dark. This vacillating, shady situation and action may be interpreted in terms of both its physical and its metaphorical (spiritual, intellectual, sexual) meaning. Since the narration centers on Edna, who is descended from Kentucky Presbyterians, a subtle (if partially blasphemous) religious reference might be inferred from the title as well. Edna's awakenings, from sleep to life and from dreams/reveries to rationality, endow the narration with a vague sense of transience. Her prevailing and pervasive characteristic is one of potentialities not wholly actualized, of stages not entirely reached, of thoughts not distinctly formulated, of emotions not openly recognized.

From the outset, Edna is described as possessing liminal features.[7] She is difficult to figure in traditionally structured categories or even to be appraised by readers and fellow characters. Perhaps only Dr. Mandelet understands her. This wise and sympathetic old man invites her confidence ("I don't want you to blame yourself, whatever comes. Good night, my child")[8] and may be regarded as the foil to her self-centered and rigid father. If his paternalistic and positivistic outlook forces upon her an evaluation of reality that smothers her imaginative flutterings ("youth is given up to illusions. It seems to be a provision of Nature, a decoy to secure mothers for the race"), he is also the only character who offers to comfort and assist her in her despair. Mandelet possesses "anointed eyes," implying that he is gifted with a "di-

vine" attribute: He sees far into the unseen. (His name, incidentally, sounds like and contains a pun on "Mandalay," the mystic
bay of Burma, a symbol of Eastern wisdom.) But Edna's distinctive
condition is to be isolated and incapable of limiting (or unwilling
to limit) the extent of her finally assumed independence.

All that concerns Edna is marked by an essential state of "in-
betweenness." She can be defined mainly by approximation and is
not integrated into any milieu: neither in the one in which she was
raised nor in the one in which she lives. Physically she is "rather
handsome than beautiful"; her eyes are "yellowish brown,"
"about" the color of her hair; her eyebrows are "a shade darker."
Her figure is characterized by a "noble beauty" and a "graceful
severity," where the chiasmus of the adjectives bridges distances
and mitigates polarities. In short, Edna is "different from the
crowd." Religiously, as a child, she ran away "from prayers, from
the Presbyterian service" and, as an adult, again on a Sunday, she
leaves the "stifling atmosphere" of the Catholic mass. Intellec-
tually she is caught between an "outward existence which conforms" and an "inward life which questions." Emotionally she is
torn by conflicting "impulses" and she feels either "happy" or
"unhappy," she is either "kind" or "cold" (Chap. 26). Although
there were traces of French blood in her, we are told at the beginning of the narrative that they "seemed to have been lost in dilu-
tion"; ethnically and genetically, we might say, she is elusively
complex.

In a society regulated by convention, dress and comportment
are of utmost importance. It is revealing that, whereas the Creole
women around her wear either white (Adele Ratignolle and
Madame Lebrun) or black (the enigmatic "lady in black" and
Mademoiselle Reisz) garments and ornaments, Edna, at Grand
Isle, unites the opposites, wearing a white muslin "with a waving
vertical line of brown running through it" and, in New Orleans,
she puts on a blue dress with a red silk handkerchief around her
head and a golden satin gown.[9] The color symbolism is unmistak-
able: Edna's white, which points to a transfiguration of being, is
brought down to "earth" by brown (her eyes and hair), which
indicates matter and sadness; blue and red represent her counter-
tendencies toward abstraction and sexuality; and gold is the sym-

bol of the fully realized, supreme essence.[10] As far as behavior is concerned, at the beginning of the story, although her Creole, "feminine" friend Adele is cautious about exposing her skin to the strong rays of the sun, Edna does not protect hers at all, disclosing her defiant disregard of southern womanly taboos ("You are burnt beyond recognition," her husband had angrily exclaimed in Chapter 1, not realizing that a new, phoenixlike identity was about to rise out of her "ashes"). Above all, not fully understanding the Creole code, she makes the "unfortunate blunder" of falling in love with Robert, thus living out dramatically a relationship originally meant to be taken only as pleasantly courteous. Spatially as well, Edna cannot be surrounded by fixed, socially controlled, enclosed places. As a child, in her native Kentucky, she had walked "diagonally" (along the longest and thickest, the most toilsome but most exalting, route) across a field of bluegrass. As a grown woman in New Orleans she takes extended walks, preferring "to wander alone into strange and unfamiliar places" – a mimesis of her conditions – rather than staying at home, the home of which she says: "It never seemed like mine." She needs open, preferably vast, spaces: a meadow, the beach, the streets of a large city. Since it is the tendency of her nature to escape structured categories, her ambivalence is underlined by the characteristics of the places where events occur. She begins to understand her real self at Grand Isle, a summer resort between the city and the sea. When she feels the first "throbbings of desire" for Robert, she spends a day with him at a yet more distant and smaller island, Chenière Caminada, as if she needed to retreat to a wilder, more secluded and separated area where fantasies might reign more freely and where the two of them might pose as the living characters of a revisited fairytale. After her return to New Orleans, viewing her neighborhood with the outlook of an outsider, she judges it "very French, very foreign."

In all respects, Edna is a stranger who lives on the periphery of (in between) two ways of life – the American and the Creole, the strictly Puritanical and the sensuously Catholic – and two sets of conventions – the reserved and the exuberant. At the same time, Edna lives spiritually and logistically outside the social institution that tends to define her. She does not follow her husband to New

York; she leaves her husband's house; she entrusts her children to the care of her mother-in-law. Presumably expressing the opinion of Creole society, Adele aptly observes, "She is not one of us; she is not like us." Edna is considered to be and feels different; she finds the world around her not only "alien" but even "antagonistic."

Similarly, in the temporal dimension, the narration emphasizes the liminal time of day, the period of darkness between one day and another. In the first section of the book, situated at Grand Isle and consisting of sixteen chapters, events are grouped under six time sequences: The first (Chaps. 1–3) covers the period from one Sunday morning to Monday morning; the second (Chaps. 4–6) from an afternoon to the night of the same day; the third (Chaps. 7–8) from one morning to luncheon of the same day; the fourth (Chaps. 9–14) from a Saturday night (August 28) to Sunday night; the fifth (Chap. 15), one evening and night; and the sixth (Chap. 16), one morning in September (characteristically, a liminal month). According to the traditionally accepted[11] four divisions of the day cycle (morning, midday, afternoon, and evening/night), mornings and evenings/nights seem to be in balance (five recurrences each).[12] The most momentous events occur during the evenings/nights. On the first Sunday night (Chap. 3), Edna is abruptly awakened and upset by her husband, thus disclosing the discontent beneath the smooth surface of her married life. On the occasion of Edna's late afternoon swim in the ocean, Chopin comments fervently on Edna's quest (Chap. 6). On a Saturday evening, Edna swims far out alone for the first time and feels she is "reaching out for the unlimited in which to lose herself," thus realizing her potential for autonomy. Later that night, for the first time since her marriage six years before, she resists her husband's "compelling wishes" with determination. On the following late Sunday afternoon, at Chenière Caminada, she wakes up like Sleeping Beauty, after a long sleep (of "a hundred years," as Robert/Prince Charming tells her), to live a few hours of perfectly idyllic harmony (the most extended period in the book) in a magic atmosphere. On an evening, finally, Edna learns that Robert is leaving for Mexico and realizes that, through him, she is losing "that which her impassioned, newly awakened being demanded."

In this first section of the book, the actual time covered by the narrative is about four unconsecutive days between the middle of August and the middle of September. Semantic and thematic linguistic references link the sequences to one another;[13] each sequence (except for the fourth) starts with the day subdivision following the one that ends the previous sequence.[14] The impression of a fluid, languorous, but compact stretch of time is thus effectively created. Only the fourth sequence stands out from the third and fifth, and breaks this contiguous and predictable succession of the day cycle phases: It begins and ends at night, whereas Chapter 8 ends at luncheon and Chapter 15 starts in the evening. Covering a very important lapse of time, in which Edna learns how to swim – that is, how to enter the fluid element itself – and her feelings for Robert coalesce into a deep infatuation, it fits her character that this sequence is circumscribed by darkness.

The second section of *The Awakening* is situated in New Orleans and contains twenty-two chapters. The actual time span covered by the narrative is about five months – roughly from the end of September to the middle/end of February, which is the end of winter in this region. Since this second section runs approximately only one-third longer than the first one, time is often fragmented into sporadic but significant events, which are rarely temporally tied to the preceding or following ones. No succession of the day's four solar subdivisions is to be consistently found between one chapter and the next. Darkness prevails throughout. The section starts on an evening (Chap. 18) and ends at night (Chap. 38). The critical events that affect the protagonist happen in the evenings/nights: the third (and last) quarrel with her husband (Chap. 17), her first visit to Mademoiselle Reisz, the pianist, who plays a crucial role in the story (Chap. 21); dinner during which Dr. Mandelet realizes that Edna vibrates with life and is ready for change, and in which she recounts the just invented (and "open") anecdote of the two lovers who disappeared in a pirogue; the sense of absolute freedom and rest she experiences when everybody (the four men in her life: her father, husband, and two sons) leaves her and, alone, she reads Emerson (Chap. 24); Alcée's kiss, which affects her like "a flaming torch"; her regret that "it was not the kiss of love which had inflamed her" (Chap. 28); her sumptuous dinner party in which, as will be shown, so much is revealed (Chap. 30); the beginning of her affair with Alcée that very night (Chap. 31); her first kissing of Robert (Chap. 36); her assistance during Adele's childbirth and her realization that a woman's independence is hindered by the existence of her children (Chap. 37). Finally, that very night, there is the shattering of all her dreams and illusions by the farewell note from Robert. In ten chapters the main action occurs in the evenings/nights (Chapters 17, 21, 23, 27, 28, 30, 31, 34, 37, 38) and in six (Chapters 20, 24, 25, 26, 33, 36) it starts in the afternoon. Only in Chapters 18, 22, 29, and 35 do events occur in the mornings, and in two chapters (19 and 32) they cover diverse days and times.

In the third section, which consists only of Chapter 34, the action rapidly returns to Grand Isle for the span of half a day and the time is toward noon, the moment of fullest sun and splendor.

Edna's inner crisis comes to a head because of her infatuation/love for Robert, who shares some of her physical and psychological characteristics, which are achieved both by making her more masculine and him more feminine. "In coloring he was not unlike his companion," writes Chopin. "A clean-shaved face made the resemblance more pronounced."[15] Psychologically, too, Robert tends to be passive and "childish."[16] A gallant with a reserved and delicate personality, he is so affected by the world around him that his eyes, rather than possessing a color and an expression of their own, "gathered in and reflected the light and languor of the summer day." Affinities between them – if one wants to push speculations beyond the text – date from long before their first meeting at Grand Isle: Edna and Robert were both orphans (of mother and of father, respectively) and had been brought up by the one parent who – from the evidence given in the case of the former and from what we learn in the case of the latter – did not seem to have much in common with or to have a preference for them: Edna's older sister, Margaret, is pictured as being as stern as their father, the colonel (Chap. 7 and, in passing, Chap. 22); Mademoiselle Reisz says that Aline Lebrun loves Robert's brother, Victor, more than him.

At the outset of their relationship at Grand Isle, Edna and Robert share a similar way of amusing themselves (Chaps. 1 and 2) and, above all, a propensity to conjure up and become attuned to fairy-tale situations (Chaps. 12 and 13). In Chapter 1 Chopin shows them facing each other while sitting on the step of a porch (a liminal place), and again in Chapter 4 they hold the same position. They are indeed mirror images – or doubles – of one another, thus disclosing both their haunting death instinct and their desire for immortality. When Edna sees and confronts Robert after his return from Mexico, she repeats almost verbatim[17] the sentence with which he summarizes his past months' experiences. She does this in order for him to realize (although he does not) how in harmony they have been, notwithstanding their separation. Only appar-ently, however, are her additions to his sentence *minor* specifica-tions ("Caminada," "sunny," "with a little more comprehension than") or reservations ("still"). In effect, they indicate how atten-tive she has been to the events that stirred her life from the sum-mer on. In particular, when talking of their fairytale interlude, she gives the magic little island (Grand Terre) its complete name to emphasize its importance in her life. She describes the old fort as "sunny" to convey to him some of her own feelings of that memo-rable day when she had thought that "she would like to be alone there with Robert, in the sun," the symbol of plenitude. Informing him that in the city she had tried to give her life meaning by working, she asserts that the occupation she had undertaken was not just "mechanical." But immediately afterward she has to ad-mit that she has not succeeded in her intent, possibly because – as we know from previous authorial comments – she is "devoid of ambition, and striving not toward accomplishment." Even if they share many characteristics, then, Robert, after five months and a sojourn abroad, is very much the same man he was when he left: timid, tied to the rules of his milieu. Edna, on the other hand, has tested herself in new personal as well as professional directions and has begun to realize that dreams and fantasies should not be fettered by institutional forms. At their second encounter she can "maternally" reproach him by saying: "You have been a very, very foolish boy, wasting your time dreaming of impossible things. . . . I give myself where I choose."

Their state of in-betweenness is further exemplified by Edna's and Robert's being the middle members of a feminine and a masculine triad. (Three is a recurrent number throughout the narration.)[18] Edna is both pulled toward and repulsed by Adele Ratignolle – the devoted mother, the Madonna, the Queen – on the one side, and, on the other, by Mademoiselle Reisz – the devoted pianist, the disagreeable and ugly spinster. As a girl, Edna had been caught between two very dissimilar, strongly defined, assertive sisters: Margaret, who was "matronly and dignified" and Janet, who was "a vixen." Now she is attracted by Adele and Mademoiselle Reisz for different reasons. Dissimilar as they are, Adele, sensuous and placid, helps Edna think of herself as a "woman," whereas Mademoiselle Reisz, malicious and imperious, "seemed to reach Edna's spirit" through her "divine art," thus helping her to think of herself as an "individual."

Robert stands between and is juxtaposed to both Leonce Pontellier, the acquisitive businessman and boring husband, and Alcée/Victor, the physically attractive and morally unscrupulous men about town. Robert shares features with and is different from both: Like Leonce, he is dependable and conventional, but he is also imaginative and agreeable. Like Alcée/Victor, given his resemblance to Edna, he is handsome (though his physical aspect is never fully described) and successful with women, but he is also a tactful gentleman.

Both Edna and Robert represent transitional states of being, states marked by ontological mobility and epistemological vagueness. Edna is often defined by negations (or, as we have indicated, by approximations). Psychologically, her husband thinks that she is "not a mother-woman." She feels "not thoroughly at home in the society of Creoles" because she is "not accustomed to an outward and spoken expression of affection." Deprived of a mother, Edna could not fully be a daughter and is not moved by any sisterly affection. She refuses to attend her younger sister's wedding. She is also prone to abandon her responsibilities as a wife: After the third quarrel with her husband, she flings her wedding ring upon the carpet and stamps her heel upon it (Chap. 17); she is intensely, but even in her own eyes only occasionally, a mother, "fond of her children in an uneven, impulsive way" and "It was with a wrench and a pang that Edna left her children. . . . All along the journey homeward their presence lingered with her like the memory of a delicious song. By the time she had regained the city the song no longer echoed in her soul."

Only "half" of Edna is where the whole person should be: She is often "half-awake"; she feels "half-hearted"; she traces "half remembered experiences"; she cherishes the "half-darkness" of her garden; she can at times only "half comprehend" what is said. She is also "absent-minded" and lacking in "forethought," because she acts upon impulses and whims, which she only "half" knows. In this, too, she differs greatly from the Creole attitude toward life which seems to be marked by a monotonous consistency (Leonce's devotion, Chap. 3) and an annoying persistence (Adele's conversation, Chap. 4). Further, Edna possesses only half of what, according to Mademoiselle Reisz, is needed to be an artist: the natural talent but not "the courageous soul. . . . The soul that dares and defies." She seeks a total (spiritual, intellectual, sexual) love relationship, but is torn between a romantic fantasy (Robert "had seemed nearer to her off there in Mexico") and an erotic liaison (after sensuously responding to Alcée's first kiss, she regrets that "it was not love which had held this cup of life to her lips"). Stamped by ambivalence, she is portrayed in her final act as still both dying and alive.

Edna's mind and body are literally trying to catch up with each other. Following the exaltation provoked by her first solitary swim, walking home, she feels "as though her thoughts were elsewhere — somewhere in advance of her body, and she was striving to overtake them." Upon leaving Adele's house, before her final plunge into the sea, she again feels "as if her thoughts had gone ahead of her and she was striving to overtake them." At the beginning and toward the end of the narrative, these two comments underline Edna's still unachieved completeness of being. Only in the water does she experience a fusion of body and soul, because in the formal-informal element she loses her *principium individuationis* and her physical self seems to become as light and free and "weightless" as her spiritual self.

Edna's "symbol" is the maze suggested, first, by the depths of the sea (Chap. 6) and, later, by the "deep tangle" of the garden outside her New Orleans house. In Chapter 7, and briefly again in Chapter 34, the sea is specifically related to the "green" Kentucky meadow of "blue grass." After her last quarrel with her husband, she finds solace in looking out at "the dusky and tortuous outlines of flowers and foliage. She was seeking herself and finding herself in just such sweet, half darkness which met her moods." Through the adjectives, "green" and "blue," two expanses (the *blue* sea and the *green* garden) are connected with the third one (the *green* meadow of *blue* grass): It is only when these two colors (the natural and the spiritual) merge that Edna feels happy ("entertained") and would like to remain in that situation, as in a labyrinth, "forever."

Linguistic structures underscore the thematic ambiguity of the book. An adverbial clause is often used to approach, albeit tentatively, Edna's inner self: "as if" (or "as though"). In trying to define what Edna thinks or, more frequently, what Edna feels,[19] Chopin often reverts to this hypothetical, circuitous, basically unreal adverbial clause to relate her character's inner world to the outside one. "As if" establishes, according to Vaihinger's analysis, "an apperceptive construct under which something can be subsumed and from which deductions can be made," although what is stated in the conditional clause is considered unreal. This formula posits the "subjective" validity (and not the objective significance) of judgment, since the assumptions are presented as only imaginary.[20] Thus, for instance, Chopin informs us that Edna's eyes would be held on an object "as if lost in some inward maze of contemplation or thought." Edna tells Adele that on that momentous summer day in Kentucky, when walking through the meadow of blue grass, she threw her arms out "as if swimming." The day she goes to Chenière Caminada with Robert, she acts "as if she had placed herself in alien hands." When she visits Madame Ratignolle with her sketches and drawings, she confesses that she feels "as if I wanted to be doing something," and, when alone in her husband's house, she is overcome by exultation and walks through it "as if inspecting it for the first time." On melancholy days it seems to her "as if life were passing by, leaving its promise broken and unfulfilled." After her reaction to Alcée's kiss she feels "as if a mist had been lifted from my eyes." When by chance she meets Robert for the second time in New Orleans, in the cafe in the little garden, she reacts "as if a designing Providence had led him into her path." After kissing Robert, she looks into his face "as if she would never withdraw her eyes more." Edna's epistemological self is presented as so frail in its relationship with reality that she cannot conceive real analogies or draw actual equivalences; she can articulate only hazy, tentative comparisons that seem to have no objective significance and to be rooted in no objective reality. The validity, the expediency of such significances and such realities, is, however, admitted by the very possibility (or necessity) of the comparisons themselves. Edna's cognitive process is thus based on *fiction;* she approaches reality through a potentially rich but dangerously indirect method. She yearns for abstractions, for illusions created by her "mythical" impulse: "the abiding truth," "the unlimited in which to lose herself," "life's delirium," "the unattainable."

Transitional states are inevitably states of inner and outer ambiguity. In her quest for her true self, Edna loses, or enhances with the addition of the opposite ones, her original gender connotations and social attributes. At Grand Isle she becomes so attached to Adele Ratignolle – who possesses "grace and majesty" and speaks "the law and the gospel" – that she looks at her "like a faultless Madonna," with the feeling with which, in Provençal times, a man would have looked at a woman. Adele is even described as "the fair lady of our dreams," with "spun-gold hair," blue eyes that resemble "sapphires," and lips "so red one could only think of cherries." To such a goddess or fairytale figure, Edna cannot but be tied by the subtlest of bonds, or what "we might as well call love." As Edna conquers areas within and outside herself for the expression of her individuality (she goes out freely, she paints, she shuns her obligations, she lives alone, she takes a lover whom she does not love, she is ready to start an affair with another one whom she loves), she gradually abandons the prescribed "womanly" manners. She talks "like her father," she drinks like a man ("She drank the liquor from the glass as a man would have done"), she twice defines her own attitude as "unwomanly," and, taking the initiative, *she* kisses her beloved Robert. Symbolically, at the end of the narrative, she stands alone in the nude, on the seashore, like the man whose figure her mind had once evoked when listening to a piece of piano music: "There came before her imagination the figure of a man standing beside a desolate rock on the seashore. He was naked. His attitude was one of hopeless resignation as he looked toward a distant bird winging its flight away from him." Becoming independent and living freely entails, for Edna, possessing and developing androgynous characteristics. Chopin seems here to imply that an up-to-date goddess and a fairytale or romance protagonist should be both feminine and masculine (not like Adele, who, being only "feminine," is a "bygone heroine").

In her first published short story, "Wiser Than a God" (1889), Chopin had pitted the artistic profession against family life. Paula Von Stoltz,[21] the main character, thinking of these two vocations as mutually exclusive, chooses to become a famous pianist, that is – paraphrasing the words of the epigraph[22] – to "be wise" *rather than* "to love."

In *The Awakening,* to love/to be in love is a means *toward* becoming wise, a stage toward realizing one's "position in the universe," toward metamorphosing into the "god" who is possibly the only being capable of matching these two faculties. Having started her quest with the desire to love and to be loved, Edna ends it by subsuming her capacity to live and becoming wise. In her last moments, when she is back on the beach at Grand lsle, she realizes that, although she would like to have Robert near her, "the day would come when he, too, and the thought of him would melt out of her existence, leaving her alone." But her love is, at last, directed to the prime sources of being: the sea and the sun, that is, both to the ambivalent, mediating agent that includes the formal and the informal and to the all-encompassing spirit of creation. In this final scene she is indeed both the real woman and the imagined man. And since she feels like "some new-born creature opening its eyes in a familiar world that it had never known," her/his plight becomes that of reconciling opposites, of coming to terms with mysterious essences (a "familiar" and yet "never known" reality), by achieving plenitude. By overcoming gender restrictions, by breaking all barriers, by identifying life and death, Edna attains, at the very end, a precarious, quasi-divine wholeness.

122

Symbols of negative meaning are interspersed with positive ones. Edna is not, like Paula Von Stoltz, wiser than a god, but for a short while she is as wise as the gods/goddesses who might also love. First by emphasizing Edna's similarity to Robert and then by making her drop all social, "feminine" niceties, Chopin creates an androgynous being whose dynamic tension must be kept in balance. Such a complex and compound entity alone can master, in her/his awareness (and with the complicity of the indeterminate ending), inner and outer limits. Through her androgyny Edna succeeds in achieving the wholeness of a composite unity, both integral and versatile, both necessary and free. Triumphing over sex and role differentiations ontologically implies subjugating that which substantiates but curtails, and ethically it entails mastering the grim unilaterality of responsibility. The bourgeois crisis[23] that Edna endures – the discrepancy between duty toward others and right toward herself, between social demands and personal yearnings, between repressive order and chaotic freedom – may be overcome in the grasped fullness of her dual being.

If we are tempted to regard Edna's last gesture as narcissistic (the drowning and the water symbolism imply as much), the fact that she abandons her self points rather to a reaching out for, an attainment of, more self. She merges with that supreme reality and *other* cosmos that has "no beginning and no end," in which opposites are not so much reconciled as potentially summed up, and birth, death, rebirth are endlessly recycled in the Heraclitean flux. At this point she can cast "the unpleasant pricking garments from her." Although "faded," these garments stand for the worn-out social rules and the hypocritical allure behind moralistic conventions, and even for the illusion of completeness through sexual encounters ("pricking"). On the verge of attaining wholeness, Edna can throw aside "that fictitious self which we assume like a garment with which to appear before the world." These garment metaphors take on greater drama from the fact that clothes metaphors play so large a role in the narration. After Robert's departure for Mexico, her existence had already appeared to her "like a faded garment which seems to be no longer worth wearing." And after having assisted Adele – when she still believes that Robert is waiting for her at home – she regards the turmoil of her fierce emotions as "a somber, uncomfortable garment, which she had but to loosen to be rid of." By divesting herself of all her garments – her bathing suit, but also her "outer" fictitious self, her past experiences and her wrenching emotions – she frees herself from her physical life, logical thoughts, and subconscious perceptions, as well as from external hindrances, in order to enter a condition of authenticity and joy in the water under the sun. Through a baptismal immersion in the sanctifying waters of inner grace, and in the face of immortality symbolized by the bees and sun, she is platonically recapturing that lost innocence that is her soul,[24] cloaked and hampered by the body and its trappings. The scene and the imagery recall those at Christ's baptism on the Jordan (Matt. 3:16–17). Unlike the episode in the Gospel, however, there is here no saintly witness, no official recognition, to testify to Edna's essence, and the bird hovering above has "a broken wing" and is therefore not an adequate symbol of the divine. Once again, Edna retains her ambiguity by being *alone* to intuit and interpret the cosmic event of which she is the protagonist: her super-natural awakening.

Only twice before, in the first section at Grand Isle, had Edna been shown on the beach in the morning: in Chapter 7, in which she discloses moments of her inner life to Adele for the first time, and in Chapter 16, in which, under Mademoiselle Reisz's eyes, she plunges and swims "with an abandon that thrilled and invigorated her." In both cases the combination of water and sun prompts important insights into herself: By recalling an episode of her childhood, she realizes her propensity to abandon herself to a vast natural solitude (the meadow of bluegrass). By reacting with a plunge in the water to an unpleasant piece of gossip (in the past, Robert had been interested in Mariequita, the pretty and spontaneous, "natural" Spanish girl), she again abandons herself to another vast natural solitude (the sea). At the end, not only does she identify sea and meadow ("the water was deep, but she lifted her white body and reached out with a long, sweeping stroke. . . . She went on and on . . . thinking of the bluegrass meadow"), but she lets herself be seduced by the sensuous "touch of the sea" under the sun, that is, under the most powerful symbol of intuitive knowledge, of the spirit in its highest individual realization, in its "illumination."[25] Since, moreover, the sun, like the sea, symbolizes the beginning and the end of all, we are confronted with a scene in which each distinct element and their combination underscore the notion of an eternal cycle of birth, death, and rebirth. No longer under the influence of the moon, the passive and "feminine" symbol[26] – and, incidentally, also a symbol of death – Edna is here in conjunction with the sun, the golden divinity, the symbol of eternal life. The influence of the moon, which had presided over her gradual development, is thus overcome. In this final scene, at the "mercy" of the sun, if her body will die, her Life will not perish.

Encircled by the night, she for a while arises to the sun's level during her farewell dinner party (Chap. 30). Wrapped in the golden "shimmer" of her satin gown, at the head of a table covered with pale yellow satin and adorned both by "massive brass candelabra, burning softly under yellow silk shades" and by yellow roses, with champagne glittering in the crystal glasses, Edna suggests "the regal woman, the one who rules, who looks on, who stands alone."[27] In the profusion of gold that is the sun's basic attribute, one may say that she represents the sun/Apollo's nightly counterpart (the moon/Artemis). In the crucial Chapter 10, while going to the beach the night in which she learns how to swim, she already misses Robert "just as one misses the sun." Not in juxtaposition to, however, but in merging with those parts of being that compose her unity will Edna finally attain a sense of completeness.

In the last scene, no longer attached to ephemeral life, Edna enters a love relationship with the sun and the sea, the primal elemental factors; after experiencing "how delicious" it feels to stand naked under the sky, she lets herself be embraced by the water. In the process of attaining fulfillment with Nature, with the Emersonian Not-Me, with the universe, the reality of her life is left behind and the people she was related to (sons, husband, friends, relatives, beloved one, and even her secretly treasured first love) become distant and meaningless. Back at Grand Isle, finally rejecting both absolute renunciation (in the first section of the book represented by the lady in black) and juvenile fulfillment (previously incarnated by the two young lovers), she opts for absolute fulfillment.

It is consistent with what we regard as the author's deliberate decision not to propose definitive answers and not to assign precise and restricting qualities to Edna that the book ends when she is achieving the wholeness for which she craves. For this reason, although in the last scene Edna is imbued with a mystic aura, negative or deathly forces are also at work: Mademoiselle Reisz's sneer, her father's and her sister Margaret's (undoubtedly harsh) voices, the barking of an old dog (the animal psychopomp), the sycamore tree (which traditionally protects the souls of the dead),[28] the metallic, hideous clang of the cavalry officer's spurs. To the end Edna must remain poised between contrary visions, messages, and meanings in order to retain her polyvalent nature. Her wanderings do not end because the maze, her symbol, has led her into the cavern where she undergoes a change of heart and where a superior *being* emerges. The only "cavern" she had been familiar with is one "wherein discords wailed." In this last scene, therefore, in the composite center of her being, Spirit and Nature, Reason and Understanding, I and Not-I do merge for a chronologically brief, but symbolically infinite, time. In this merging, Edna joins the source of *Being*. She lives and dies within the twisting labyrinth, which stands for the perennial cycle of life–death–rebirth. The process of becoming – following the two main patterns of the labyrinth – is, indeed, infinite like the spiral, and perpetually returning on itself like a braid.[29] The ambiguous ending permits an open and intersected interpretation: Death and life may be regarded as phases of a single existence, either of which will be superseded by the other.

From a rationalist outlook, by presenting both of these possibilities concurrently, Chopin has courted misunderstanding. Her transcendentalist influences, however, justify her diffidence toward ordinarily accepted standards of judgment and solely rational explanations. In her epistemological relativism, she allows neither naturalistic conditions nor purely logical procedures to account for the mysterious complexities of life. As she had once written: "truth rests upon a shifting basis and is apt to be kaleidoscopic."[30]

Whitman's impact on Chopin has already been analyzed, particularly on her imagery and symbolism.[31] What must be noted is her debt to Emerson and the transcendentalists with respect to her sense of human beings as intermediaries between myth and consciousness, between the projections of their "divine" unconscious (dreams, visions, intuitions) and their interpretations of such projections, by which "Feeling is converted into thought; intuition, into insight."[32] In this perspective, human beings serve a dynamic function of intercommunication and interchange, and perform a role that shuns the law of conceptual logic as well as the gratifications that come from strict definitions. This inner potential connects the individual with those dried-up ("shrunk") powers that, as Emerson claims in *Nature,* had once peopled the cosmos with gods born of his/her unconscious "overflowing currents. Out from him sprang the sun and the moon; from man, the sun; from woman, the moon. The laws of his mind, the periods of his actions externalized themselves into day and night, into the year and the seasons."[33]

In a very unobtrusive and apparently unconscious manner, Chopin appears to have seized upon mythic figures to help unravel both the complexity and the mystery of human existence. As with so many artists, gods and goddesses are thus employed by her as hypostases of a higher unity. Writers often resort to myths not as ways to escape history, but as structures "for dealing with shared crisis of self-definition in the face of the unknown";[34] in such cases, myths offer them the opportunity of "naming the unknown."[35] Chopin may have kept a related group of myths (and of gods and goddesses) more or less intentionally[36] in mind – without meticulously following them in every detail – to depict her protagonist's mystifying identity. The mythical content may also account for the open ending.[37]

Edna's spiritual tendencies are hinted at from the beginning of the book. The first thing we know about her is that she possesses a physical emblem of spirituality, "strong, shapely hands." (One recalls Mandelet's "anointed eyes": His name may refer also to the French word for hand.) Leonce Pontellier, who considers his wife "a valuable piece of personal property," regards his possessions as "gods." Furthermore, the images of portals and of a temple are employed to convey what marriage was for Edna: "As the devoted wife of a man who worshiped her, she felt she would take her place with a certain dignity in the world of reality, closing the portals forever behind her" (Chap. 7). And again: "Within the precincts of her home she felt like one who has entered and lingered within the portals of some forbidden temple." But she, the pantheistic goddess, suffocates "inside" the *reality* of married life, conceived of as a temple that entombs her. She has to fling open the portals onto *realities* of dreams to be herself, to capture her divinity: "Edna began . . . to feel again the realities pressing into her soul." Her dreaming and daydreaming indicate a preference for the inner world and are conducive to tearing down those barriers that, in the "awakened" state, do not allow her archetypal models to surface. Thus, mythic and fairytale figures perfectly suit Edna, who has become the heroine of her dreamed about, compelling romance from the moment when the "mystic spirit" brought her to the "realms of the semicelestials."

In the languorous tempo and hazy atmosphere of the first section of the book, and in the fragmented tempo and tense atmosphere of the second section, there are two moments (Chapters 13 and 30) in which the protagonist is not only different from but "above" all the other characters.

In Chapter 13 Edna acts and speaks like fairytale princesses – like Sleeping Beauty or Snow White: "The whole place was immaculately clean, and the big, four-posted bed, snow-white, invited one to repose. It stood in a small side room. . . . Edna, left alone in the little side room, loosened her clothes. . . . [She] stretched herself in the very center of the high, white bed. How luxurious it felt to rest thus in a strange, quaint bed." Later, she speaks like Sleeping Beauty: "How many years have I slept?" she inquired. "The whole island seems changed. A new race of beings must have sprung up, leaving only you and me as past relics." "You have slept precisely one hundred years." In both fairytale heroines, the awakening to individuality (and to sexuality) occurs after a period of withdrawal from active life.

At another time (Chap. 30) Edna takes on attributes of Persephone, the queen of the underworld, the goddess who crosses continuously the threshold of life and death: the sceptre (suggesting the regal woman who rules), a tiara of diamonds ("Something new, Edna?" exclaimed Miss Mayblunt, with lorgnette directed toward a magnificent cluster of diamonds that sparkled, that almost sputtered, in Edna's hair, just over the center of her forehead"), the pitcher (Edna does not actually pour the libations, but cocktails and champagne enrich and brighten her table), the color yellow.

The most important connection between the two fairytale princesses and the mythic queen is that both Snow White/Sleeping Beauty and Persephone share the motif of the long sleep, similar to death (for the Greeks, Sleep and Death were divine brothers). Edna sleeps and often takes naps even during the day, as if to balance her sleeping and waking hours. The two princesses and Persephone, after a period of sleep and isolation, will awake (be reborn) and experience joy and completeness, either with the prince or with the mother. In the last scene, after her long phase of semiactivity and narcissistic "contemplation of the self"[38] – of semisomnambulism – Edna is finally enjoying ecstasy in Nature. The two fairytales may be regarded as the popular version of the myth of Persephone,[39] who lives, in some variants, six months on earth (from March – approximately the month in which Edna returns to Grand Isle – to August – the month in which Edna first appeared at Grand Isle) and six months in Hades (from September to February, the time Edna spends in New Orleans). In both the fairytales and the myth, the theme is that of cyclical birth–death–rebirth.

In Chapter 30, however, a number of reticulated suggestions are offered to give substance and depth to the mythical figure of Persephone. At Edna's dinner party, oriental refinements are conjured up to create a voluptuous setting: the music of mandolins (an instrument that derives from the oriental lute and, incidentally, contains another reference to the hand, and therefore to spirituality), the perfume of jessamines (the Arabic flower), the splash of a fountain (the heart of the Arabic garden).[40] In this context, Victor, Robert's younger brother, a *"tête montée,"* is expressly depicted as Dionysus, the oriental-Greek god of "intoxicated delight."[41] On his black curls, in fact, is laid a garland of roses (not of ivy, however – but roses are possibly more suggestive) and "his dusky eyes glowed with a languishing fire." One of the women guests drapes a white silk scarf "across the boy in graceful folds," and another one makes him sip champagne from a glass brought to his lips. At this moment of the night, a "mystic cord" seems to pass around Edna's guests and "jest and laughter" bind them together in a sort of repressed bacchanal. (By these hints Chopin suggests a Swinburnean atmosphere.)[42]

Through his physical appeal and the impetuousness of his nature, Victor gains Edna's and the other women's sympathies. Up to that point in the narrative he has played a minor role: He has mainly been shown bickering with various people: his mother, Mr. Farival (Chap. 15), and – as Madamoiselle Reisz recounts – with Robert (Chap. 16). Victor is now at the center of everybody's attention and turns into "a vision of Oriental beauty." The oriental (sensual, exotic, even cruel)[43] role is so well enacted by him that in the last chapter of the book, at Grand Isle, he teases Mariequita and makes her jealous of his acquaintances and deeds in the city by telling her that the women at Edna's feast were "youthful houris."

Dionysus is the chthonian god of oriental origin who, like Persephone, stands for the two main cycles of nature: death and rebirth, winter and spring, barrenness and fertility. Indeed, in the Orphic tradition, he was believed – as Dionysus Zagreus – to be the son of Zeus and Demeter, Persephone's mother. He, the divine child, the twice born, belongs to both the world and the underworld; he is the god of duality. Dionysus is, in his masculine and feminine nature, a formidable synthesis of opposites[44] and a link between disparate realities. He represents paradox and the embrace of mad ecstasy that occurs when death and life meet.[45] One of his familiar settings is the sea, and the sea is Victor's special domain, since he spends most of the year at Grand Isle. Dionysus/ Victor has, therefore, affinities with Persephone (and the "semi-celestial" Ariadne)/Edna.

It has been stated before that Robert and Edna share important psychological and physical traits and that they function in similar ways within the narrative. If Edna possesses and brings into play characteristics usually considered masculine, Robert possesses feminine ones. He is youthful and attractive, but he is also endowed with self-control and balance. In a phrase, he represents the man of conscience. From the mythological point of view, Robert (whose name in German etymology means "bright") is thus comparable to Apollo, the ambidextrous god of circular completeness (symbolized by the sun disc). Confronted with Dionysus, Apollo stands as his opposite, but also as his complement. They epitomize "the eternal contrast between a restless, whirling life and a still, far-seeing spirit."[46] At Delphi the two gods were celebrated as juxtaposed divinities: Apollo during the solar months, Dionysus in the winter. Moreover, Dionysus excites some of the very faculties that Apollo guards: prophesying, singing, playing musical instruments. Robert confesses that in Mexico "Something put into my head that you cared for me, and I lost my senses," thus guessing the truth, and after the trip to Chenière Caminada, he sings the melody "Si tu savais" with a voice that is "not pretentious" but "musical and true." In the summer, at Grand Isle, we see little of Victor; in the winter, except at the end, when spring is advancing, Robert is away in Mexico.

Dionysus is often represented as accompanied by processions of Maenads and satyrs; on three occasions (Chaps. 9, 15, 30) Victor is portrayed at the dinner table, surrounded by a big, vociferous company of men and women. Victor is the only man, in addition to Robert, to walk with Edna under her sunshade (Chap. 20), thus showing a certain degree of possible intimacy with her.[47]

The bond that unites Victor, Robert, and Edna is subtle but so strong that when, at the party, Victor kisses the palm of Edna's hand, she is moved because "The touch of his lips was like a pleasing sting." Robert will react in a similar way when Edna kisses him: "She leaned over and kissed him – a soft, cool, delicate kiss, whose voluptuous sting penetrated his whole being." The "sting" of a wasp or bee, combined with "pleasing" and "voluptuous," suggests a masochistic combination of pain and delight, Thanatos and Eros. The bee, incidentally a solar symbol, is identified with Persephone's mother (Demeter), and represents the resurrection of the soul and the sacred Word (significantly, the bee reappears at the very end of the book). Victor, Edna, and Robert, therefore, share the same divine substance, the Spirit.[48]

Victor (Latin, "winner") is the youngest of the men to flirt with

Edna: He is nineteen, Alcée's age when he was wounded in a duel in Paris. The two men personify, in fact, the impetuous roué, the "wicked, ill-disciplined boy," who completely fulfills the demands of his temperament (the number nineteen, as the result of the sum of ten and nine, indicates both a complete cycle and full human satisfaction).[49] "Alcée" may refer to Alcaeus, the Greek poet who celebrated convivial and physical pleasures, and his surname, Arobin, sounds like "Arab" and points toward exoticism and sensuality.

In *Die Geburt der Tragödie (The Birth of Tragedy)* (1872), Nietzsche had ascribed the conditions of great art (as those operative in Greece in the fifth century B.C.) to a blending of the Apollonian and the Dionysian principles, the former described as the world of visions and rapt repose and the latter as the world of voluptuousness and strenuous becoming. Even if Chopin did not know Nietzsche's work,[50] these mythological dichotomies were widely discussed,[51] and indeed seem to be incarnated in the two Lebrun brothers. (Their surname refers to matter and sadness, to earth and death.) One may also hazard that in the serene contemplation and joyful ecstasy of her final musical[52] and dramatic merging, Edna symbolizes their union.

Dionysus and Persephone are like the children of Demeter, and Dionysus and Apollo are, respectively, a chthonian and a solar double. In our context, if Victor and Edna are similar because both are defined as impetuous (Chaps. 30 and 32), Robert and Edna are more than just doubles of one another. They are similar and *almost* coeval: We are obliquely informed[53] that he is twenty-six, whereas, when the narration starts, Edna is twenty-eight. They may thus bring to mind the famous divine twins, Apollo and Artemis, who were born of Leto under a palm tree. When, in the first scene of the book, Edna and Robert are together, she is fanning herself with a palm leaf (Chap. 2).

In several traits Edna may be linked to Persephone, the queen of Hades. In her beauty and fertility she is a chthonian Aphrodite, who, in turn, is an immortal Ariadne (even the name of the daughter of Minos of Crete is associated with that of the love goddess).[54] In other traits, however, she may be regarded as being

132

analogous to Artemis, the virgin goddess. Artemis is associated with the moon and has a virginal, independent nature. Edna is represented mainly during the dark times of the day and declares that she will not be hampered by her children: "I would give up the unessential; I would give my money, I would give my life for my children; but I wouldn't give myself." Artemis, moreover, delights in wild nature and performs the function of protectress of childbirth. Edna likes open, solitary, "uncivilized" places and rushes to assist Adele at the end, notwithstanding the presence of Robert in her house. Not being a mother-woman, Edna's two past experiences of childbirth seem to her "far away, unreal, and only half-remembered" (Chap. 36). It is as if, like most goddesses (Hera, for instance), after her own childbirths, she had returned to a virginal state: She tends toward a life of complete independence and craves "solitude" (Chaps. 4, 6, 9, 10, and 34). Artemis loves dogs; at the beginning of her experience of marital independence Edna plays with her children's little dog (Chap. 24) and at the end she hears the barking of an old dog (Chap. 39). In her desire to cast manners and obligations aside, Edna may thus be considered wild and ruthless, like Artemis. Finally, Artemis, the Lady of Clamors, is associated not only with Apollo but also (like Ariadne) with Dionysus,[55] thus bringing Edna, Robert, and Victor mythologically even closer together.

In trying to account for all the aspects of such an elusive character as Edna, we realize that neither Persephone nor Artemis entirely encompasses her. Yet another goddess, the one who completes the triad of the virginal ones, is necessary: Athene (who, being present with Artemis at Persephone's abduction, indicates her affinity with them). To adopt Richard Ellmann's term, Chopin does not proceed "singlemythedly." The reference to so many contiguous archetypes may be justified by the composite nature of Edna's personality, which, to be fully accounted for, needs a plurality of figures. But they are tightly connected to one another, notwithstanding their particularities.

Dumezil has maintained that a tripartite system representing the three functions of productivity, force, and sovereignty is to be found in Indo-European myths.[56] In our text, productivity would be embodied in Persephone, force in Artemis, and sovereignty in

Athene. Athene is characterized by a complete independence of humanity. Edna says to Robert, "I give myself where I choose," and in the last scene she thinks, "Today it is Arobin; tomorrow it will be someone else." Athene, like Artemis, performs the role of protectress of childbirth, but, above all, of the arts. Edna is endowed with gifts as a painter. Furthermore, Athene embodies the inner tension of being both a virgin and a mother. Such an antithetical condition is well represented by Edna's split between the psychological and the physiological levels of her existence. Masculine maiden and virgin mother, Athene is essentially androgynous and, as such, all the more similar to Edna. The goddess is often associated with the snake or serpent, a symbol of autochthony and a messenger between the underworld and human reality.[57] This reminds us of Edna's first swim, when the sea "swelled lazily in broad billows that melted into one another and did not break except upon the beach in little foamy crests that coiled back like slow, white serpents." In the final scene too, "The foamy wavelets curled up to her white feet, and coiled like serpents about her ankles." The serpent represents rebirth, renewal, and spiritual enlargement in the inner world.

Another animal sacred to Athene is the horse, which is also one of Apollo's attributes (a further, indirect connection with Robert). Chopin writes that "There were possibly a few track men out there who knew the race horse as well as Edna"; and when Dr. Mandelet compares her to "some beautiful sleek animal waking up in the sun," he may be thinking of a horse. Athene has connections both with Dionysus, to whom according to one tradition, she was related,[58] and with her half-brother Apollo, who, according to another secret tradition,[59] was thought of as her son by Hephaistos. In the richness of her multiple aspects, Athene is thus involved with the two main mythical figures behind the two most important male characters in the novel.

Athene is intimately bound to Persephone. In fact, the owl, a symbol of wisdom, is an animal they share.[60] After her first quarrel with her husband at Grand Isle, when Edna goes out on the porch and first becomes aware of "some unfamiliar part of her consciousness," all is silent around her "except the hooting of an old owl." The similarity between Athene and Persephone is attested to

134

by still another symbol of fertility: the pomegranate for Athene and the orange (the internal structure of which is similar to that of the pomegranate) for Edna. On two eventful occasions she is pictured among the orange trees. First, in Chap. 13, she appears four times among or under the orange trees, to emphasize the abundance of feeling that takes hold of her at Chenière Caminada (the first part of the island's name may recall the oak and its mushroom, symbols of longevity and of regeneration through death).[61] Later, in Chap. 36, while sitting under the orange trees of the small cafe in the garden, Edna meets Robert just before their reciprocal declaration of love in her pigeon house.

The plurality of mythical figures needed to portray such an elusive character as Edna points to the discontinuities of the self that, according to Bloom,[62] typically characterize American romanticism. At the same time, however, Chopin seems to direct attention to the most discerning elements that link these figures to one another in order to lend Edna her many-sided uniqueness. Athene is, for instance, the protectress of feminine handiworks, in patriarchal times represented by the spindle or the needle. In popular fairytales these are often fairies' or witches' tools. In "Sleeping Beauty," the princess pricks her finger with the old woman's spindle in the tower and falls asleep. At the opening of "Snow White," after pricking her finger with a needle, the queen longs for a child to whom she indeed gives birth not very long after. The sexual implications of these tools[63] stress the role of Athene and of middle-aged or old women as go-betweens (midwives) in a psychological (as well as a physical) sense. Such females may display either the positive or the negative sides of womanhood, like the seven good fairies versus the eighth, wicked one in "Sleeping Beauty" or the queen mother versus the wicked stepmother in "Snow White."

In *The Awakening,* two women without men (a widow and a spinster) are invested with a similar function. Aline Lebrun and Mademoiselle Reisz live in high, tortuous, dark, gothic eyries. Madame Lebrun's room at Grand Isle "was situated at the top of the house, made up of odd angles and a queer, sloping ceiling" and Mademoiselle Reisz's apartment in New Orleans is under a roof and is full of "dingy" windows, which admit "a good deal of smoke and soot"; from them "the crescent of the river" and "the masts of ships and the big chimneys of the Mississippi steamers" can be seen. These two women are the benevolent fairy and the malevolent witch, respectively: Madame Lebrun is always dressed in white, works at her sewing machine with the determination with which Mademoiselle Reisz practices her piano art, and is still "a fresh, pretty woman." Although of little importance in the narrative, Madame Lebrun is the mother of the two most important men and the one who, by providing Edna with Mademoiselle Reisz's address, indirectly favors Edna's and Robert's meeting in New Orleans. Mademoiselle Reisz, by contrast, is always dressed in black and, without being malevolent (although her surname rhymes with "vice"), is certainly wry, critical, and prophetic. Soot and chimneys belong to witches as well as to her, as does the shining crescent. But it is "the crescent of the river" and not of the moon. This shift underlines the fact that Mademoiselle Reisz cannot be associated with the most pregnant symbol of woman's fertility. Witches' horror of water (therefore of the spiritual element) is also characteristic of her: "Mademoiselle Reisz's avoidance of the water had furnished a theme for much pleasantry." Her physical aspect, moreover, is rather grotesque: "Her laugh consisted of a contortion of the face and all the muscles of the body," her hands have "strong, wiry fingers." She is so small and deformed that at Edna's dinner party she has to be "elevated upon cushions," and when she sits at the piano, "the lines of her body settled into ungraceful curves and angles." She always wears "a batch of rusty black lace with a bunch of artificial violets pinned to the side of her hair." Like witches, Mademoiselle Reisz is ageless and might be as old as her furniture, "dingy and battered from a hundred years of use" (the number underlines the mythic time in which she, like a character in a fairytale, lives).[64] Everything in her points toward the magic being who stirs up hidden forces. It is, for instance, after Reisz's playing of the piano that Edna, passionately moved by it, swims for the first time alone. It is she who quiets Edna's troubled soul with her music. She is the first to tell Edna that Robert is in love with her and, finally, she sharply conveys to her that Robert is not the person whom she should love: "If I were young and in love I should never deem a man of ordinary caliber worthy of my devotion." Conversely, it is to Mademoiselle Reisz that Edna first discloses both her desire to leave her husband's house and her resolution "never again to belong to another than herself"; moreover, it is to her that Edna first confesses her love for Robert (Chap. 26).

Mademoiselle Reisz is thus a conjurer and a *ficelle,* a necessary link that accounts both for Edna's gradual awareness of her aspirations and for the progress of the action. (Edna will meet Robert again in Mademoiselle Reisz's apartment.) She may be connected to Athene (and Edna) because, in her dark side, the goddess wears the head of one of the gorgons, the terrible Medusa, on her aegis, her shield. Mademoiselle Reisz's head is obviously not covered with serpents, but the author insists on her unusual millinery, her only characterizing ornament.[65] If, with her talent and her dedication, Mademoiselle Reisz stands for the spiritual urge forward, this urge, as in the case of the gorgon, is perverted by an excessive, presumptuous, ultimately self-destructive turning on itself.[66]

Since the pursuit of a rigid coherence is advocated by Chopin neither in professional nor in family life, Adele, too, takes on for a while the semblance of Medusa in the last scene in which she appears − that of the delivery of her child: "Her face was drawn and pinched, her sweet blue eyes haggard and unnatural. All her beautiful hair had been . . . coiled like a golden serpent." Even Adele, the tender mother, the sweet and sympathetic Madonna, who, as Demeter tried to protect Persephone, would like to protect Edna ("In some way you seem to me like a child"), shows her dark side. Demeter, too, becomes Demeter Erynnis.[67]

In Athene/Medusa, therefore, the three different characters of Edna, Mademoiselle Reisz, and Adele merge, at least temporarily. So that if we might have been tempted to detect in the characterization of Mademoiselle Reisz and, to a lesser extent, of Aline Lebrun traces of the old patriarchal prejudice that rejects women without men as anomalies, with Adele as Medusa as well, another subtle indication can be inferred: In a repressive society,[68] sooner or later, continuously or occasionally, womanhood as such is destined to be regarded, even by a woman artist, as frightening (possibly because the female Medusa forces men and women to look at themselves and realize their true nature). By drawing a many-sided character like Edna, Chopin has bridged the gap between the two more stereotyped opposing figures of Adele and Mademoiselle Reisz, while imbuing them with unexpected, linking attributes.

Other evidence throws light on the controversial meaning of the book. Pallas Athene is the moon[69] (and, as such, is connected with Artemis) and represents the lunar cycle. The Panathenaea Festival, which every four years celebrated magnificently the protectress of Athens, could begin on the twenty-eighth of the month dedicated to her.[70] When *The Awakening* begins, Edna is twenty-eight, and the only precise date in the whole narration is that of Edna's first swim: August 28. Twenty-eight is the number that indicates the lunar months and is closely related to the female. It is the arithmetic sum of the first seven numbers and represents a complete cycle, totality, eternal life, thus fitting the etymology of Edna's name, which means "rejuvenation" in Hebrew[71] (and is close to Erda, the German earth goddess). Through a perennial cycle of birth–death–rebirth she is, therefore, true to her name. What is of special interest to us is that twenty-eight points to a dynamic perfection.[72]

August 28 is also, however, the day on which the Christian calendar celebrates Saint Augustine, the Church doctor who would have agreed with the Holy Spirit in not vouchsafing to any woman a significant amount of wisdom (to paraphrase Chopin's words in Chapter 6). Augustine, as we know, was deeply influenced by Plotinus's *Enneads,* which identified the content of true wisdom in self-direction and self-awareness in knowledge of the Good. In Plotinus's thinking, when man reaches freedom in the One, he is freed from all dependence, from all individuality: The return to unity marks his return to transcendent independence when he is finally alone with the Alone,[73] when he attains "self union." Only by transcending oneself, by becoming all things, through a pantheistic union with the Universal Being does one attain infinity, perfection. Augustine insists on the gulf (the word, so rich in metaphorical meanings, makes us think of the Gulf at Grand Isle) between man and God, but retains the neoplatonic belief that redemption as well as regeneration proceeds by turning inward upon oneself and that obligation to God entails a desire for self-fulfillment. He maintains that duty and self-interest ultimately

138

coincide, because love of self and love of God, even if they exist separately, are coextensive.[74]

In the mystery surrounding Edna's last act, one may detect concepts and posit hypotheses that afford a multilateral dimension to her instinctual decision, especially since, when walking toward the sea, "She was not dwelling upon any particular train of thought." Even the fact that the narrative ends with Chapter 39 may offer a subject for speculation. The result of thirteen multiplied three times, this number symbolizes a dynamic, limited, and relative system tending to the acquisition of a more forceful potentiality. Being elevated to the third power, the system strives toward perfection, totality.[75]

With her inner and outer liminality, her search for existential fulfillment and her multifaceted, goddesslike traits, Edna entices us, moves us. Whatever judgment we will pass on her struggle for independence and self-realization – that is, no matter how doomed from the start is this bourgeois myth propounded by a society that then denies it for women – through her final sensuous and mystic ecstasy, seeking immersion in her environment, she either purges herself of her narrowly conceived individualism or exorcises the isolation into which she was cast.[76] Rather than living as under a "narcotic" – etymologically associated with "sleep" and with Narcissus – she breaks the isolation of her existence, sublimates her instincts by directing them toward the Ideal, and joins the universe.

Edna's plight is constrained by neither social circumstance nor obstacle. She is left free to do as she pleases: She has no husband, no children, no relatives, no acquaintances, no society either, overtly to malign or brutally to hamper her. From the aesthetic point of view, the writer neither attempts to project an intriguing situation by adopting involuted narrative structures nor does she care to reveal to the fullest extent her characters' deepest psychological instincts and motivations. Yet we are conquered by Edna's *naiveté*[77] and by the sheer honesty of her timeless, solitary quest.

NOTES

1. Gabriel Germain, *Chants pour l'Ame de l'Afrique* (Paris: Debresse, 1956), p. 89: "L'homme qui a une âme n'obéit qu'à l'Univers."

139

2. In Chapter 32, the protagonist feels that "She began to look with her own eyes; to see and to apprehend the deeper undercurrents of life. No longer was she content to 'feed upon opinion' when her own soul had invited her."

3. In Chapter 38, Edna says: "I don't want anything but my own way."

4. Carol P. Christ, *Diving Deep and Surfacing: Women Writers on Spiritual Quest* (Boston: Beacon Press, 1980).

5. George M. Spangler, "Kate Chopin's *The Awakening:* A Partial Dissent," *Novel* 3(3) (Spring 1970):249–55; and Jane P. Tompkins, "*The Awakening:* An Evaluation," *Feminist Studies*, 3(3–4) (Spring–Summer 1976):22–9.

6. The title of the book was actually meant to consist of both the present one and the one that the author had originally proposed to the publisher: *A Solitary Soul*. Per Seyersted, *Kate Chopin: A Critical Biography* (Baton Rouge: Louisiana State University Press, 1969), p. 221, n. 38.

7. See Victor W. Turner, "Betwixt and Between: The Liminal Period in Rites de Passage," in *The Forest of Symbols: Aspects of Ndembu Ritual* (Ithaca, N.Y.: Cornell University Press, 1967), and also "Passages, Margins, and Poverty: Religious Symbols of *Communitas*" in *Dramas, Fields, and Metaphors: Symbolic Action in Human Society* (Ithaca, N.Y.: Cornell University Press, 1974). To be liminal entails achieving a new state of being, a new spiritual *communitas*, whereas to be marginal implies being permanently excluded, an absolute "other." It is the aim of this chapter to try and demonstrate that Edna belongs to the liminal.

8. For instance, Edna thinks of herself as a child and as childish (Chaps. 7, 19, 35, 39), and is defined as a child by Adele Ratignolle (Chap. 33), by Doctor Mandelet (Chap. 38), and by the author (Chap. 10).

9. Edna wears the red silk handkerchief on her head after having kissed Alcée, that is, after having begun to break the moral code of her class. The sexually free Spanish girl, Mariequita, is the only other character to wear a red piece of clothing, in fact, a red kerchief on her head (Chap. 12).

10. For a discussion of the meaning of these colors, see Jean Chevalier and Alain Gheerbrant, *Dictionnaire des Symboles* (Paris: Laffont, 1969), pp. 107–9, 126, 111–12, 663–5, 564–6, respectively.

11. Ibid., p. 436.

12. Five mornings are expressly mentioned: the Sunday morning at the beginning of the story; the following Monday morning (Chap. 3); one morning (Chap. 7); one Sunday morning (Chap. 12); one morn-

ing (Chap. 16). Five evenings/nights are accounted for: the first Sunday night (Chap. 3); one evening (Chap. 5); one Saturday night, August 28 (Chaps. 9, 10, 21); one Sunday night (Chap. 14); one evening and night (Chap. 15).

13. The first sequence is connected to the second one by both a linguistic and a thematic reference ["A few days later a box arrived for Mrs. Pontellier from New Orleans" (Chap. 3), and "She was sitting there the afternoon of the day the box arrived from New Orleans" (Chap. 4)]. The second sequence is connected to the third one by the use of an identical background: the sea at Grand Isle. (At the end of Chapter 5 Edna swims in the sea, and in Chapter 6 the author comments on her swimming. At the beginning of Chapter 7, while contemplating the sea, Edna starts thinking about herself, thus beginning to realize the nature of her personality.) The fourth sequence appears to be tenuously connected to the one that precedes it (at the beginning of Chapter 9 the author informs us that the time is a Saturday night "a few weeks after the intimate conversation held between Robert and Madame Ratignolle," which occurred in Chapter 8). This sequence is not linked to the following one. The fifth sequence is tied to the sixth one by a thematic reference – in Edna's flashback – to Robert's leaving "five days ago" (Chap. 16).

14. The first sequence ends (Chap. 3) in the morning (and an afternoon is anticipated); the second sequence starts (Chap. 4) in the afternoon and ends (Chap. 6) at night; the third sequence starts (Chap. 7) in the morning and ends (Chap. 8) at luncheon; the fourth sequence, instead, starts (Chap. 9) at night and ends (Chap. 14) at night; the fifth sequence starts in the evening and ends at night (Chap. 15); the last sequence (Chap. 16) starts in the morning.

15. Edna notices that his hair is "the color of hers" (Chap. 33).

16. Adele Ratignolle says to Robert: "You speak with about as little reflection as we might expect from one of those children down there playing in the sand" (Chap. 8). The author comments, "He was childishly gratified to discover her appetite" (Chap. 13). Later Edna defines him as "a foolish boy" (Chap. 34). When Robert is not in the company of women, he likes to be with children (Chaps. 2 and 7).

17. Robert says: "I've been seeing the waves and the white beach of Grand Isle, the quiet, grassy street of the Chenière, the old fort at Grand Terre. I've been working like a machine and feeling like a lost soul. There was nothing interesting." Edna says: "I've been seeing the waves and the white beach of Grand Isle, the quiet, grassy street

of the Chenière Caminada, the old sunny fort at Grand Terre. I've been working with a little more determination than a machine, and still feeling like a lost soul. There was nothing interesting."

18. For instance, three are the quarrels between Edna and her husband (Chaps. 3, 11, 17); three are her visits to Mademoiselle Reisz (Chaps. 21, 26, 33); three times the lady in black appears with the lovers (Chaps. 7, 8, 15); three times she appears with the lovers and Mr. Farival (Chap. 12). Three times the twins play the piano (Chaps. 1, 2, 9). Before marrying, Edna had experienced three infatuations (Chap. 7). Robert speaks three languages (Chap. 2). Linguistically, too, the narration is dotted by triads: When Edna is shattered by the news that Robert is going to Mexico, she desperately wonders how he could leave so suddenly, "as if he were going over to Klein's or to the wharf or down the beach." The colonel reproaches Edna for her "filial," "sisterly," and "womanly" wants (Chap. 24); Arobin may be met at "horse courses," "operas," or "clubs" (Chap. 25). Robert sweetens his coffee with three lumps of sugar (Chap. 36). Celina's husband is defined as "a fool, a coward, and a pig" (Chap. 39). Three is the first perfect number, which represents totality, the achievement of divine Unity, the participation of humanity in the invisible world. It is also associated with the search for one's biological and sexual identity.

19. In several cases the adverbial clause, when referring to Edna, is preceded by the verb "to feel." For instance: "I felt as if I must go on forever" and "I feel this summer as if I were going through the green meadow again" (Chap. 7); "a feeling of exultation overtook her as if some power of significant import had been given her to control the working of her body and her soul" (Chap. 10); "Edna felt as if she were being borne away from some anchorage which had held her fast" (Chap. 12); "she felt as if she were thoroughly acquainted with him" (Chap. 23); "I feel as if I had been wound up to a certain pitch – too tight – and something inside of me had snapped" (Chap. 31).

20. Hans Vaihinger, *The Philosophy of "As if"* (London: Routledge and Kegan Paul, 1968), pp. 93, 95.

21. This young woman, whose vocation is to become a concert pianist, and Mademoiselle Reisz do not bear French surnames. Perhaps on account of their exacting calling, the author prefers to assign them ancestry different from that of most of the other, more "easygoing," characters.

22. "To love and be wise is scarcely granted even to a God."

23. In Adorno's dialectical analysis, the narrowly conceived *principium*

individuationis is one of the myths of bourgeois ethics that, distancing "truth" and "freedom" from the social context and imbuing authenticity with "religious authoritarian pathos without the least religious content," further alienates the "monadological" individual. Theodor W. Adorno, *Minima Moralia,* trans. E. F. N. Jephcott (London: Verso, 1978), pp. 152–5. These Marxist observations may be of help insofar as they emphasize how tightly *The Awakening* is connected to the bourgeois tradition and culture.

24. The word "soul" occurs more than twenty times in the narrative, four times in each of the following chapters: 6, 21, 39; in this last, the contexts in which the word was used in the previous two chapters are repeated.

25. Chevalier and Gheerbrant, *Dictionnaire des Symboles,* pp. 710–14.

26. Ibid., pp. 474–8.

27. In Sandra M. Gilbert's "The Second Coming of Aphrodite: Kate Chopin's Fantasy of Desire," *Kenyon Review* 5(3) (Summer 1983), Gilbert argues that Chopin is portraying in Edna a *fin-de-siècle* Aphrodite, thus "exploring a vein of revisionary mythology allied not only to the revisionary erotics of free love advocates like Victoria Woodhull and Emma Goldmann but also to the feminist theology of women like Florence Nightingale . . . and Mary Baker Eddy" (61).

28. Chevalier and Gheerbrant, *Dictionnaire des Symboles,* pp. 197–201, 728.

29. Ibid., pp. 445–7.

30. Kate Chopin, "Emile Zola's '*Lourdes*'" (1984) in *The Complete Works of Kate Chopin,* ed. Per Seyersted, 2 vols. (Baton Rouge: Louisiana State University Press, 1969), Vol. 2, p. 697.

31. See Seyersted, *Kate Chopin,* pp. 86, 151; Lewis Leary, "Kate Chopin and Walt Whitman" in *Southern Excursions: Essays on Mark Twain and Others* (Baton Rouge: Louisiana State University Press, 1971), p. 170; Joan Zlotnick, "A Woman's Will: Kate Chopin on Selfhood, Wifehood, and Motherhood," *Markham Review* 3 (October 1968):1–5; Gregory L. Candela, "Walt Whitman and Kate Chopin: A Further Connection," *Walt Whitman Review* 24(4) (December 1978):3.

32. Jeffrey Steele, "Interpreting the Self: Emerson and the Unconscious," in *Emerson, Prospect and Retrospect,* ed. Joel Porte (Cambridge, Mass.: Harvard University Press, 1982), p. 102.

33. *The Collected Works of Ralph Waldo Emerson,* ed. Robert E. Spiller and Alfred R. Ferguson (Cambridge, Mass.: Harvard University Press, 1971), vol. I, p. 42.

34. Estella Lauter, *Women as Mythmakers, Poetry and Visual Art by Twentieth-Century Women* (Bloomington: Indiana University Press, 1984), p. 8.

35. Albert S. Cook, *Myth and Language* (Bloomington: Indiana University Press, 1980), p. 1.

36. A. Pratt maintains that women writers often resort to myths as acts of discovery prompted by imagination and intuition. Annis Pratt, *Archetypal Patterns in Women's Fiction* (Bloomington: Indiana University Press, 1981). In the plan of studies of Chopin's convent school, mythology was one of the subjects taught. Louise Callan, *The Society of the Sacred Heart in North America* (New York: Longmans, 1937), pp. 735–6.

37. Myth has, among its features, that of being an "expanding contextual structure." Eric Gould, *Mythical Intentions in Modern Literature* (Princeton, N.J.: Princeton University Press, 1982), p. 177.

38. Bruno Bettelheim, *The Uses of Enchantment. The Meaning and Importance of Fairy Tales* (New York: Knopf, 1977), p. 226. Chopin is obviously indebted to the romantic tradition on sleep and dreams. She could not have known Freud's *Die Traumdeutung (The Interpretation of Dreams),* which appeared in 1900 and was not translated into English until 1913, yet her work shows a profound sensitivity to the nature of the unconscious.

39. Marie L. von Franz, *The Feminine in Fairy Tales* (Irving: University of Dallas, 1972), pp. 18–43. The following Jungian analysis is based on the conviction that – as Bickman observed – Jungian psychology completes the movement of American romanticism and turns "metaphysics into a phenomenology of consciousness. The most striking activity in American Romanticism is that . . . of the imagination exploring those areas where ideas are felt as well as thought, and where spiritual aspirations and sexual desires are discovered to spring from the same inner dynamics." Martin Bickman, *The Unsounded Centre: Jungian Studies in American Romanticism* (Chapel Hill: University of North Carolina Press, 1980), p. 39.

40. Curiously, when looking at the garden earlier (Chap. 17), Edna had not mentioned this fountain. Chopin's narrative method is often based on reticence and understatement. For example, one learns the names of Edna's children (Raoul and Etienne) in Chapters 3 and 14, respectively; again, only in the last chapter does one first learn that during the previous summer, Edna had always tripped over some loose planks in the porch.

41. Walter F. Otto, *Dionysus, Myth and Cult* (Dallas: Spring Publications, 1981), p. 65.

42. Margaret Culley, "Edna Pontellier: A Solitary Soul," in *The Awakening, An Authoritative Text, Contexts, Criticism*, ed. M. Culley (New York: Norton, 1976), p. 227. See also Gilbert, "The Second Coming of Aphrodite," 61.

43. Victor, who insists on singing the song Edna does not want to hear, provides the disruptive climax of the party.

44. Otto, *Dionysus, Myth and Cult*, p. 136.

45. Ibid., p. 137.

46. Ibid., p. 208.

47. Edna appears under the sunshade twice with Robert (Chaps. 1 and 12) and once with Adele (Chap. 7).

48. Chevalier and Gheerbrant, *Dictionnaire des Symboles*, pp. 1–2.

49. Ibid., pp. 292–3, 531–3.

50. In *Kate Chopin, A Critical Biography*, Per Seyersted never mentions Nietzsche as a possible influence on Chopin. But Daniel S. Rankin in *Kate Chopin and Her Creole Stories* (Philadelphia: University of Pennsylvania Press, 1932, p. 174) suggests that this novel may have been indebted to Gabrielle D'Annunzio, as well as to other representatives of European aestheticism. Specifically, he mentions *The Triumph of Death* (translated into English in 1896), which shows the impact of Nietzsche and of Wagner. In both novels there is indeed a strong emphasis on the power of music to move and to reveal the inner world of every human being. Incidentally, in a book published posthumously in 1901, *Der Wille zur Macht (The Will to Power)*, Nietzsche writes that Dionysus is the epitome of "transitoriness" and declares that he can be interpreted "as enjoyment of productive and destructive force, as *continual creation*." Friedrich Nietzsche, *The Will to Power*, ed. Walter Kaufmann (New York: Vintage Books, 1968), p. 539, sects. 1049, 1885–6. It is, of course, too early to speak of a Nietzschean influence here. Although Nietzsche's books began appearing in the 1870s, his influence on Anglo-American culture did not commence until 1896, when, newly translated in Britain, his works started to be known. Patrick Bridgwater, *Nietzsche in Anglosaxony* (Leicester: Leicester University Press, 1972), p. 150. For further reference, see Stephen Donadio, *Nietzsche, Henry James, and the Artistic Will* (New York: Oxford University Press, 1978). Nietzsche is linked to American culture through his devotion to Emerson. From 1862 and for more than a quarter of a century, "Emerson was the object of

Nietzsche's continuing interest." Herman Hummel, "Emerson and Nietzsche," *New England Quarterly* 19 (1946):73. It is possible that the occasional Nietzschean theme in Chopin is actually Emersonian and one acquired on native ground.

Note that Walter Pater, too, had studied the figure of Dionysus as the expression of a power that is "bringing together things naturally asunder, making, as it were, for the human body a soul of waters." W. Pater, "A Study of Dionysus," in *Greek Studies, A Series of Essays* (London: Macmillan, 1922), p. 29.

51. For a complete bibliography of Nietzsche, see Herbert W. Reichert and Karl Schlechta, *International Nietzsche Bibliography* (Chapel Hill: University of North Carolina Press, 1968).

52. Kate Chopin, *The Awakening*, ed. with an introduction by Lewis Leary (New York: Holt Rinehart, 1970), pp. 12–13.

53. In Chapter 5 the author gives us his age indirectly: We have to make an addition (fifteen plus eleven) in order to know it. Edna's age, instead, is stated twice (Chaps. 6 and 30).

54. Otto, *Dionysus, Myth and Cult*, pp. 181–8.

55. Ibid., p. 92. Incidentally, Ariadne (who, like Persephone, Artemis, and Aphrodite, belongs to the element of moisture, Becoming, and death) had, like Edna, two sons.

56. Georges Dumezil, *Myths et Epopée*, 3 vols. (Paris: Gallimard, 1968).

57. Karoly Kerenyi, *Athene, Virgin and Mother in Greek Religion* (Zurich: Spring Publications, 1978), pp. 17, 55–7. Given Chopin's familiarity with the poetry of A. C. Swinburne, see his "Erechtheus."

58. Ibid., p. 47.

59. Ibid., p. 54.

60. Ibid., p. 32.

61. Chevalier and Gheerbrant, *Dictionnaire des Symboles,* p. 169.

62. Harold Bloom, *Poetry and Repression: Revisionism from Blake to Stevens* (New Haven, Conn.: Yale University Press, 1976), p. 255. The critic maintains that "The Emersonian or American Sublime . . . differs from the British or the Continental model not by a greater or lesser degree of positivity or negativity, but by a greater acceptance or affirmation of discontinuities in the self."

63. Von Franz, *The Feminine in Fairy Tales*, p. 38.

64. The number ten (or its multiples: one hundred, one thousand, ten thousand) is frequently employed in the book. Ten designates a totality in movement, a return to unity, an alternation, or better, a coexistence, of life and death. Chevalier and Alain Gheerbrant, *Dictionnaire des Symboles*, pp. 292–3.

65. To signify the alliance between rationality and vital powers, all pagan mother-goddesses carry the serpent as an attribute (Isis, Demeter, Athena, Cybele). In Christian iconography, the serpent is, instead, crushed under Mary's foot. In Medusa the serpents stand for perverted power. See S. Freud's essay "The Uncanny" (1919) and Tobin Siebers, *The Mirror of Medusa* (Berkeley: University of California Press, 1983).

66. Chevalier and Gheerbrant, *Dictionnaire des Symboles*, pp. 388–9.

67. Carl G. Jung and Karoly Kerenyi, *Essays on a Science of Mythology, The Myth of the Divine Child and the Mysteries of Eleusis*, Bollingen Series (Princeton, N.J.: Princeton University Press, 1973), p. 126. Edna and Adele are designated as "cruel" by Robert (Chap. 36) and Doctor Mandelet (Chap. 38), respectively.

68. A. Goodwin Jones, *Tomorrow Is Another Day: The Woman Writer in the South, 1859–1936* (Baton Rouge: Louisiana State University Press, 1981), p. 173–7.

69. Kerenyi, *Athene, Virgin and Mother in Greek Religion*, p. 59.

70. Ibid., pp. 40–1. Incidentally, the month dedicated to Athene corresponds to our mid-July–mid-August period, roughly both the month in which *The Awakening* begins and the "eighth" one in our calendar.

71. A similar meaning (rejuvenation, cyclical restoration) is involved in Edna's desire to eat fish. In fact, by taking her last "swim" she may become like a fish, and further, take on the nature of the supreme christological symbol. On the other hand, the fish may also symbolize her sensitivity, inconstancy, and desire to let herself go. Chevalier and Gheerbrant, *Dictionnaire des Symboles*, pp. 617–19.

72. Ibid., pp. 806–7 and 411–12. Twenty-eight, being also the sum of twenty and eight, stands for God, the primary Unity, and for resurrection and transfiguration. Twenty-eight is also the sum of the years of the Farival twins, who seem to be perfectly symmetrical (Chap. 9) and, therefore, indicate the possibility of surmounting multiplicity by attaining unity through a balanced duality. Twenty-eight, finally, designates Adam Kadmon, the Universal Man.

73. Plotinus, *The Enneads*, trans. Stephen MacKenna, rev. B. S. Page (London: Faber and Faber, 1956), particularly Enneads IV and VI.

74. See Oliver O'Donovan, *The Problem of Self-Love in St. Augustine* (New Haven, Conn.: Yale University Press, 1980). Such concepts may have been handed down to Kate Chopin through Emerson, or she may have absorbed them through her Catholic unbringing. To the impact of Augustine's doctrines (and of Plotinus's pantheism) on Puritan theology and, through it, on transcendentalism, Perry Miller has de-

voted numerous essays. His "From Edwards to Emerson" is precious, even if it studies a chronologically more limited span of theological thought. Perry Miller, *Errand into the Wilderness* (Cambridge, Mass.: Harvard University Press, 1956).

75. Chevalier and Gheerbrant, *Dictionnaire des Symboles*, pp. 766, 772–5.

76. Siebers, *The Mirror of Medusa*, pp. 57–86.

77. See Ruth Sullivan and Stewart Smith, "Narrative Stance in Kate Chopin's *The Awakening*," *Studies in American Fiction* 1(1) (Spring 1973):62–75; Cynthia Griffin Wolff, "Thanatos and Eros: Kate Chopin's *The Awakening*." *American Quarterly* 25(4) (October 1973):449–71; and Allen F. Stein, "Kate Chopin's *The Awakening* and the Limits of Moral Judgment," in *A Fair Day in the Affections: Literary Essays in Honor of Robert B. White, Jr.*, ed. Jack D. Durant and M. Thomas Hester (Raleigh, N.C.: Winston Press, 1980).

Notes on Contributors

Andrew Delbanco is Professor of English at Columbia University. His most recent work is *The Puritan Ordeal: Becoming American in the Seventeenth Century*, to be published in 1988 by Harvard University Press.

Michael T. Gilmore, Professor of English at Brandeis University, is the author of *The Middle Way* (1977) and *American Romanticism and the Marketplace* (1985). He has also edited collections of essays on *Moby-Dick* and on early American literature and published numerous articles on eighteenth- and nineteenth-century American writers.

Cristina Giorcelli is Professor of American Literature at the University of Rome. She directs the Anglo-American portion of the quarterly journal *Letterature d'America* and has published articles on such writers as Irving, Poe, Melville, James, Crane, and Stein.

Wendy Martin is Professor of American Literature at Queens College, City University of New York, and at the Claremont Graduate School. Her books include *An American Sisterhood: Feminist Writings from the Colonial Times to the Present* (1972) and *An American Triptych: The Life and Work of Anne Bradstreet, Emily Dickinson and Adrienne Rich* (1984). She has published numerous articles on American women writers and since 1972 has served as editor of *Women's Studies: An Interdisciplinary Journal*.

Elaine Showalter is Professor of English at Princeton University. Among her books on women writers are *A Literature of Their Own: British Women Novelists from Brontë to Lessing; These Modern Women: Autobiographies of American Women in the 1920s;* and, as editor, *The New Feminist Criticism*. She is currently working on a history of American women writers.

Selected Bibliography

The text of *The Awakening* for this volume appears in Per Seyersted's *The Complete Works of Kate Chopin*, published in 1969 by Louisiana State University Press, Baton Rouge. *The Awakening* was originally published in 1899 by Herbert S. Stone & Co.

Allen, Priscilla. "Old Critics and New: The Treatment of Chopin's *The Awakening*," in *The Authority of Experience: Essays in Feminist Criticism*, ed. Arlyn Diamond and Lee R. Edwards. Amherst: University of Massachusetts Press, 1977, pp. 224–38.

Arms, George. "Kate Chopin's *The Awakening* in the Perspective of Her Literary Career," in *Essays on American Literature in Honor of Jay B. Hubbell*, ed. Clarence Gohdes. Durham, N.C.: Duke University Press, 1967, pp. 215–28.

Arner, Robert. "Kate Chopin," *Louisiana Studies* 14 (Spring 1975):11–139.

Berggren, Paula A. "A Lost Soul: Work without Hope in *The Awakening*," *Regionalism and the Female Imagination* 3 (Spring 1977):1–7.

Bonner, Thomas, Jr. "Kate Chopin: An Annotated Bibliography," *Bulletin of Bibliography* 32 (July–September 1975):101–5.

Cantwell, Robert. "*The Awakening* by Kate Chopin," *Georgia Review* 10 (Winter 1956):489–94.

Chametzky, Jules. "Edna and the 'Woman Question,'" in *The Awakening: An Authoritative Text, Contexts, Criticism*, ed. Margaret Culley. New York: Norton, 1976, pp. 200–1

Culley, Margaret. "Edna Pontellier: 'A Solitary Soul,'" in *The Awakening*. A Norton Critical Edition, ed. Margaret Culley. New York: Norton, 1976, pp. 224–8.

Davidson, Cathy N. "Chopin and Atwood: Woman Drowning, Woman Surfacing," *Kate Chopin Newsletter* 1 (Winter 1975–6):6–10.

Eble, Kenneth. "A Forgotten Novel: Kate Chopin's *The Awakening*," *Western Humanities Review* 10 (1956):261–9.

Fletcher, Marie. "The Southern Woman in the Fiction of Kate Chopin," *Louisiana History* 7 (1966):117–32.

150

Forrey, Carolyn. "The New Woman Revisited," *Women's Studies* 2 (1974):37–56.

Gilbert, Sandra M. "The Second Coming of Aphrodite: Kate Chopin's Fantasy of Desire," *Kenyon Review* 5 (1983):42–56.

Jasenas, Elaine. "The French Influence in Kate Chopin's *The Awakening*," *Nineteenth-Century French Studies* 4 (Spring 1976):312–22.

Jones, Anne Goodwyn. "Kate Chopin: The Life Behind the Mask," in *Tomorrow is Another Day: The Woman Writer in the South, 1859–1936.* Baton Rouge: Louisiana State University Press, 1981, pp. 135–82.

Justus, James H. "The Unawakening of Edna Pontellier," *Southern Literary Journal* 10 (Spring 1978):107–22.

May, John R. "Local Color in *The Awakening*," *Southern Review* 6 (Fall 1970):1031–40.

O'Brien, Sharon. "Sentiment, Local Color, and the New Woman Writer: Kate Chopin and Willa Cather," *Kate Chopin Newsletter* 2 (Winter 1976–7):16–24.

Potter, Richard H. "Kate Chopin and Her Critics: An Annotated Checklist," *The Bulletin – Missouri Historical Society* 24 (July 1970):306–17.

Rankin, Daniel S. *Kate Chopin and Her Creole Stories.* Philadelphia: University of Pennsylvania Press, 1932.

Ringe, Donald A. "Romantic Imagery in Kate Chopin's *The Awakening*," *American Literature* 43 (January 1972):580–8.

Rocks, James E. "Kate Chopin's Ironic Vision," *Louisiana Review* 1 (Winter 1972):11–20.

Rosen, Kenneth M. "Kate Chopin's *The Awakening*: Ambiguity as Art," *Journal of American Studies* 5 (August 1971):197–9.

Seyersted, Per. *Kate Chopin: A Critical Biography.* Baton Rouge: Louisiana State University Press, 1969.

Skaggs, Peggy. "Three Tragic Figures in Kate Chopin's *The Awakening*," *Louisiana Studies* 13 (Winter 1974):345–64.

Spangler, George M. "Kate Chopin's *The Awakening*: A Partial Dissent," *Novel* 3 (Spring 1970):249–55.

Springer, Marlene. *Edith Wharton and Kate Chopin: A Reference Guide.* Boston: G. K. Hall, 1976.

Sullivan, Ruth, and Stewart Smith. "Narrative Stance in Kate Chopin's *The Awakening*," *Studies in American Fiction* 1 (1973):62–75.

Thornton, Lawrence. "*The Awakening*: A Political Romance," *American Literature* 52(1) (March 1980):50–66.

Tompkins, Jane P. "*The Awakening*: An Evaluation," *Feminist Studies* 3 (Spring–Summer 1976):22–9.

Toth, Emily. "The Independent Woman and 'Free Love,'" *Massachusetts Review* 14 (Autumn 1975):647–64.

Toth, Emily. "Kate Chopin's *The Awakening* as Feminist Criticism," *Louisiana Studies* 15 (1976):241–51.

Toth, Emily. "Timely and Timeless: The Treatment of Time in *The Awakening* and *Sister Carrie*," *Southern Studies* 16 (1977):271–6.

Webb, Bernice Larson. "The Circular Structure of Kate Chopin's Life and Writing," *New Louisiana Review* 6 (1976):5–14.

Wheeler, Otis B. "The Five Awakenings of Edna Pontellier," *Southern Review* 11 (January 1975):118–28.

Wolff, Cynthia Griffin. "Kate Chopin and the Fiction of Limits: 'Désirée's Baby,'" *Southern Literary Journal* 10 (1978):123–33.

Wolff, Cynthia Griffin. "Thanatos and Eros: Kate Chopin's *The Awakening*," *American Quarterly* 25 (October 1973):449–71.

Wolkenfeld, Suzanne. "Edna's Suicide: The Problem of the One and the Many," in *The Awakening*. A Norton Critical Edition, ed. Margaret Culley. New York: Norton, 1976, pp. 218–24.

Ziff, Larzer. "An Abyss of Inequality: Sarah Orne Jewett, Mary Wilkins Freeman, Kate Chopin," in *The American 1890s: The Life and Times of a Lost Generation*. New York: Viking Press, 1966.

Zlotnick, Joan. "A Woman's Will: Kate Chopin on Selfhood, Wifehood, and Motherhood," *Markham Review* 3 (October 1968):1–5.